FASHIONING THE MORE ETHICAL REPRESENTATIVE

The Impact of Ethics Reforms in the U.S. House of Representatives

Rebekah Herrick

Westport, Connecticut
London

Library of Congress Cataloging-in-Publication Data

Herrick, Rebekah, 1960–
    Fashioning the more ethical representative : the impact of ethics reforms in the U.S.
House of Representatives / Rebekah Herrick.
        p.   cm.
    Includes bibliographical references and index.
    ISBN 0–275–98018–9 (alk. paper)
    1. United States. Congress. House—Ethics.   2. Conflict of interests—United States.   I.
Title.
    JK1379.H47   2003
    328.73′072—dc21   2003042096

British Library Cataloguing in Publication Data is available.

Library of Congress Catalog Card Number: 2003042096
ISBN: 0–275–98018–9

First published in 2003

Praeger Publishers, 88 Post Road West, Westport, CT 06881
An imprint of Greenwood Publishing Group, Inc.
www.praeger.com

Printed in the United States of America

The paper used in this book complies with the
Permanent Paper Standard issued by the National
Information Standards Organization (Z39.48–1984).

10   9   8   7   6   5   4   3   2   1

Copyright Acknowledgment

The author and publisher gratefully acknowledge permission for use of the following material:

Chapter 4 is adapted from Rebekah Herrick, "Who Will Survive? An Exploration of Factors
Contributing to the Removal of Unethical House Members," *American Politics Quarterly, 28*
(2000), 96–109. Copyright © 2000 by Sage Publications, Inc. Reprinted by permission of Sage
Publications.

To my parents, Maurice and Eloise Herrick

Contents

Tables

Preface

When I first began work on this book, the House was embattled in a partisan fight over the ethical problems of Speaker Newt Gingrich (R, GA). Numerous charges were filed against Speaker Gingrich, most notably violating tax law and misleading the House about it. During the investigations, Gingrich allegedly told Minority Leader Dick Gephardt (D, MO) to "call off the 'dogs' . . . with the warning that [Gephardt] would be sorry if [he] didn't" (Gephardt, 1999, p. 201). The investigations against Gingrich continued and a complaint against Gephardt was filed with the ethics committee. Gephardt was accused but not formally disciplined for violating tax law and failing to disclose a real estate deal. Even the charges against Speaker Gingrich, some argued, were payback, since he brought charges against Speaker James Wright (D, TX) that led to his resignation. This may have been the height of the ethics climate.

The ethics climate is a time when politicians' ethics are constantly being investigated by the media, other politicians, and adjudicating arms of the government. The growth of investigative journalism and the fame and fortune reporters and news outlets received by uncovering wrongdoing on the part of politicians likely contributed to the climate. Also contributing to the climate was the political power and advantage politicians and parties could gain by going after their opponents, particularly in an era of divided government. Following the House's reprimand of Gingrich, the parties in the House agreed to limit this politics of destruction through ethics. Because of this, since the mid-1990s there have been relatively few charges filed against House members, although investigations of the executive branch during the William Clinton and G. W. Bush administrations continued, and Congress is currently investigating numerous business leaders. During the 104th Congress, fifteen members were accused of some sort of wrongdoing. Since then, there has been an average of only two members per Congress facing some sort of ethics charge. However, this relative quiet in the House may mask ethical wrongdoing on the part of members as well as continued partisan battles. In 2002, Rep. James Traficant (D, OH) became only the second member since the Civil War to be expelled after being convicted of racketeering, tax evasion, bribery, and fraud. In 2002, when Republican members threatened to bring charges against Rep. Paul Kanjorski (D, PA), who allegedly helped his nephews and daughter obtain over $9,000,000 in government contracts, Gephardt threatened to bring charges against Majority Whip Tom Delay (R, TX), and no charges were filed against either member (Bresnahan, 2002).

Given the public's and media's interest in ethics, it is surprising that Congressional scholars have not written more about members' ethics. There has been research on the causes of the ethics climate, particularly the role of the media. There has been some, albeit limited, research discussing the need for legislative ethics and how scandals affect members' reelection prospects. However, there has been even less systematic examination of the effects of the ethics climate on member retention (for those who have not been accused of wrongdoing as well as those who have), public opinion, or the ability of Congress to govern. In addition, scholars have been relatively silent as to why some members violate ethical standards and others do not. This book offers an initial exploration into the causes and consequences of the ethics climate on Congress and its members by examining a twenty-five-year period following the 1977 ethics reforms.

The basic findings of the book suggest that members have responded to the ethics climate by altering their behaviors to comply with the new standards. Although the standards are not perfect, the changes improved the legislative process. The ethics climate further improved the membership's behavior by leading to the removal of about 60 percent of the members who have been accused of unethical behavior. Although some scholars have speculated that the ethics climate harmed the public's confidence in Congress, the research presented here finds that the discovery of ethics violations had only modest negative effects on the public's approval of Congress, and most of the negative feelings were toward the membership, not the institution itself. The research also finds that ethics investigations only modestly limited Congress's ability to pass legislation. The main negative effects of the ethics climate may be in limiting the willingness of people to serve in Congress, and in limiting the ability of members who have been accused to represent their constituents and work on legislation. In addition to examining the effects of the ethics climate, the book offers and tests an explanation for why some members are more likely to violate the ethics standards than are other members. The main findings are that the members who had the opportunity to violate standards (i.e., have leadership positions, or were in the majority party), had the propensity or desire (were less wealthy, but strong party supporters), and were less likely to incur costs (had less political ambition and less well-educated voters, and won reelections easily) were more likely to violate the standards than other members. By examining who was accused and convicted of violating the standards, a bias in the system was discovered. Although leaders were more likely to be accused of wrongdoing, they were less likely to be convicted. Overall the book suggests that the reforms were generally successful in increasing the ethical behavior of members with some, albeit fairly modest, negative side effects. The standards were not perfect and the negative side effects can be reduced; thus the conclusion offers three ways to improve the process: improve the selection of members, develop a commission outside of Congress to investigate ethics violations, and punish members who make false and frivolous accusations.

Books are rarely the sole work of the author, and I would like to thank several individuals who helped me with this project. First, I would like to thank Charlie Peaden and David Doerfler for helping with the collection of data. Second, I would like to thank others who have generously shared with me data they collected for other projects. John Hibbing and Elizabeth Theiss-Morse allowed me to use their data on citizen attitudes toward Congress (see Hibbing & Theiss-Morse, 1995). In addition, Robert H. Durr, John B. Gilmour, and Christina Wolbrecht allowed me to use data they collected to also measure public opinion on Congress (see Durr, Gilmour, & Wolbrecht, 1997). Both of these data sets were invaluable for this project. In addition, I would like to thank several people who proofread, critiqued, and offered valuable suggestions on how to improve the project: David Blatt, Bob Darcy, Sam Fisher, Lori Franklin, Emily Herrick, and Sue Thomas. I also want to offer a special thanks to Michael K. Moore for his help revising and cleaning the first few chapters. Thanks are also due to John Beck who oversaw the copyediting and set the type. Finally, I thank the editors and staff at Greenwood Publishing Group.

CHAPTER 1

The Ethics Climate

Corruption, scandals, and questionable ethics decisions seem to plague the U.S. political system. Consider the following events of recent years. In the past thirty years, two presidents, Richard Nixon and William Clinton, faced impeachment charges, while two others, Ronald Reagan and George H. W. Bush, were investigated for their roles in the Iran Contra Scandal.[1] One president and one vice president resigned under clouds of suspicion.[2] Currently, Vice President Dick Cheney is being sued for possible wrongdoing in connection with his business dealings as head of Halliburton.[3] Numerous presidential cabinet members and advisors have faced allegations of unethical behavior, under which some opted to resign.[4] Others have not been nominated, withdrawn their nominations, or failed to be confirmed because of potential ethical problems.[5] As Independent Counsel Ken Starr's investigation of Whitewater figures Webster Hubbell and Susan McDougal made clear, the scope of public scrutiny now appears to extend to friends, acquaintances, and business associates of public officials.

Scandals abound in Congress as well. In 1997, Speaker Newt Gingrich (R, GA) was the first speaker to be reprimanded. While being investigated for tax fraud and violation of campaign finance laws, he misled the House. His reprimand followed just a few years after the first scandal-induced resignation of a Speaker of the House. This speaker was Jim Wright (D, TX), who left under charges of "improperly enriching himself" (Hook, 1989, p. 789). During the 1990s, the entire House was under investigation related to the post office and banking scandals from earlier in the decade, which contributed to one of the largest retirement classes in recent history. Dan Rostenkowski (D, IL), former chair of the Ways and Means Committee and arguably one of the most powerful and influential members of Congress, was defeated for reelection in 1994 amid a cloud of ethics charges, which ultimately resulted in jail time for his abuse of power to gain personal wealth. In 2002, Rep. James Traficant Jr. (D, OH) was expelled from the House after being found guilty of ten federal charges, including racketeering, bribery, and fraud (see the Glossary of Key Scandals for more details on these cases).

State and local government officials have not been immune from investigations of unethical behavior either. In recent years, the FBI has conducted successful sting operations in the California, South Carolina, Tennessee, West Virginia, Arizona, New Mexico, and Kentucky legislatures (Rosenthal, 1996). Governors and high-ranking legislative leaders have also been touched by scandal. Former Governor Fife Symington (R, AZ) left office after being convicted of bank fraud (Booth, 1997) and Jim Guy Tucker (D, AR) left the governor's mansion after being found guilty of fraudulent business practices (Schmidt, 1998). In 2002, the Wisconsin Senate Majority Leader and the speaker of its Assembly were charged with numerous counts involving misuse of their offices (Feldman, 2002).

Despite these numerous investigations for possible wrongdoings in the past few decades, the consensus among scholarly observers is that politicians have not become less ethical (Baker, 1985; Garment, 1991, introduction; Harris, 1995, chap. 2; Thompson, 1995, introduction; but see Sabato & Simpson, 1996). Instead of an increase in unethical behavior, there are simply more rules to break and more interest in investigating politicians. Several explanations have been offered for this preoccupation with ethics and allegations of wrongdoing. One reason proffered for the increased scrutiny of ethical behavior is that the media are more likely to investigate and report politicians' personal and public lives than in the past. Larry Sabato (1991, pp. 25–26) noted that the media's coverage of political events has evolved from "lap dog" journalism (1941 to 1966), a period when news media reporting primarily served the needs of the political establishment, to "watchdog" journalism (1966–1974), when investigative reporting was the norm and reporters routinely checked public officials. Watergate, the seminal event during this period, taught reporters and publishers alike the value of uncovering a scandal. During the investigation, Bob Woodward and Carl Bernstein became household names, and the *Washington Post* became a nationally recognized newspaper. Toward the end of this period, reporters began to pay more attention to the personal lives of public officials, whereas in the past they limited coverage to official actions.

The current phase of media reporting is one Sabato (1991, p. 26) terms "junkyard journalism" (1974–present). This style of journalism is marked by "harsh, aggressive and intrusive" reporting that often resembles a "feeding frenzy" where "journalists leap to cover the same embarrassing or scandalous subject and pursue it intensely, often excessively, and sometimes uncontrollably" (p. 6). The result of all this is that today's media consumer is fascinated by the dirtiest laundry, and news organizations profit by covering stories that, decades ago, reporters would not have dared to share with the public. Michael

Robinson (1994) sheds light on this change by comparing the media coverage of bribery charges against Senator Daniel Brewster (D, MD) in 1969 with coverage of similar charges against Representative Daniel Flood (D, PA) in 1978. The charges against Brewster received 170 seconds of network news coverage, while those against Flood received 4,320 seconds. Similarly, S. Robert Lichter and Daniel Amundson (1994, pp. 135–136) noted an increase in Congressional scandal coverage from 4 percent to 17 percent of Congressional news stories between 1972 and 1992. Suzanne Garment (1991, p. 288) surmised that this has culminated in a scandal machine: "The great American Scandal machine that we have built for ourselves is up and running with a ferocious momentum. It is no longer merely a tool of partisan politics. Tightened rules and beefed-up corps of investigators guarantee that we will hear a steady stream of ethics charges. Congressmen and their staffs, dependent on the media, vie to turn these accusations into public drama. News organizations, increasingly competitive, stand ready to spread the word."

The change in the media's coverage of politicians alone cannot explain the increased attention paid to political ethics. It is unlikely the media would have developed the "scandal machine" if the public was not receptive to, and indeed did not crave, reports of unethical behavior. Therefore, it is necessary that a second explanation for the increased concern with ethics focus on societal or political changes and the public's attitudes related to political ethics. Simply put, people's (in)tolerance of unethical behavior and their interest in learning about it have changed. This change in the public's interest is not entirely unrelated to changes in the media's coverage of politics. The media are believed to help shape the public agenda (Rogers & Dearing, 1988). When the media report on politicians' behavior, the public becomes aware of it. Often simply because a story is reported, the public will believe it is important. Not only have the media increased the people's interests, but the relative peace and prosperity of the end of the twentieth century may have contributed as well. In good times there are fewer absorbing issues to direct the public's attention and fewer complaints about politicians' effectiveness on the job, so there is ample time to be intrigued by stories about the character of the people in office. However, at the beginning of the twenty-first century, following the terrorist attacks on the World Trade Center and the downturn in the economy, politicians' ethics were still of concern. In 2002, Vice President Cheney was sued, Traficant was expelled, and the Senate's ethics panel admonished Sen. Robert Torrecelli (D, NJ) for accepting gifts for favors. Also in 2002, the ethics of CEOs were questioned, as several large firms had filed misleading financial statements, leading to the collapse of businesses and losses in the billions for investors.

Yet another explanation, and perhaps a better one, is that the competitive balance between the two parties at the national level encourages candidates, politicians, and political parties to draw attention to the ethical shortcomings of their opponents. Benjamin Ginsberg and Martin Shefter (1990) argue that since the electorate has become less likely to choose a single party to control the government, partisan battles over control of the government continue after elections. The party leaders are, therefore, more prone to levy charges of unethical behavior against each other. Party leaders attempt to lessen the power of the opposing party by overemphasizing and advertising the opposition's ethical missteps. Under divided governments, electoral battles no longer cease when the polls close; instead, they follow elected officials into the lawmaking arena. This political climate, which seeks to capitalize on the ethical lapses of the opposition, results in a growing frequency of investigations and the exploitation of even the slightest misstep.

Robert Roberts and Marion Doss Jr. (1997) suggest an additional reason for increased attention to ethics issues: It is politically expedient. Current political debates are frequently between anti–big government groups and the new progressives, both of which have a vested interest in finding scandals. Those working to reduce the size of the government believe big government leads to inefficiencies, waste, and corruption. Consequently, evidence of inappropriate behaviors on the part of politicians supports the claim of those hoping to downsize government. Similarly, progressives at the beginning of the twenty-first century find it in their interest to discover scandal to bolster their view that special interests are too powerful and corrupt the process. The outcome, according to Roberts and Doss, is a "public integrity war," where "innocent public servants will find themselves targets of unjustified attacks. Unethical public servants will find it possible to characterize themselves as martyrs of the public integrity war" (p. xiii).

The political attractiveness of political scandals and the media's willingness to exploit stories of ethical lapses has resulted in an increase in ethics investigations. Indeed, by the end of the Watergate scandal an "ethics climate" was thriving in the United States.[6] An effect of the heightened sensitivity to ethics issues was the institutionalization of standards of ethics in government. During the last fifty years, codes of conduct have been developed for most government employees, including members of Congress. Together the combined effects of the ethics climate and reforms have resulted in new standards of behavior for members to follow.

This book is an effort to examine the effects of the new standard of behavior created by the ethics climate and subsequent reforms on one institution: the U.S. House of Representatives. A fundamental concern for any political system is how to insure that public policy makers make decisions in the public's interest, not in their own personal interest. This concern, however, must be balanced with the need for the system to offer enough incentives that quality citizens will want to serve and that citizens can influence their elected representatives. This book explores how the ethics standards affected the ability of the House to function, including the retention and recruitment of potential policy makers. My contention is that the standards altered members' behavior in ways that improved the legislative process. Although the efforts to institutionalize the ethics standards yielded unintended consequences to the legislative process, overall these unintended consequences are surprisingly small. Nevertheless, this investigation finds areas in need of improvement and the book ends with suggestions to improve the ethics process in the House.

Throughout this book I am concerned with determining how efforts to establish, monitor, and improve the ethics standards shaped individual and institutional behaviors. This examination is focused on the *consequences* of policies designed to improve ethical behavior, not on the *causes* of the increased interest in ethical issues. This book is also not a treatise on what ought and ought not to be considered ethical behavior. I am not an ethicist, and will leave those important and weighty discussions to those who are experts in such matters.

THE IMPORTANCE OF ETHICAL BEHAVIOR
TO LEGISLATURES

Although it is not the focus of the book, some understanding of the importance of legislative ethics is needed. To understand the importance of ethical behavior for a legislature, it is necessary to define ethical behavior. According to Heywood (1997) there are three ways to define ethical behavior in governments. One type of definition focuses on societal norms. That is, socially acceptable behavior is deemed ethical; behavior found unacceptable by society is then considered unethical. Acceptable behavior for members would therefore be what society deems appropriate and would change as society changes. A second line of definitions is more normative and usually suggests that a behavior that violates democratic ideals in turn violates ethics. This approach is less relative and requires less of society. It suggests that there is an absolute ethical standard: Those behaviors which harm the democratic processes are by definition unethical. This definition of ethics illuminates their importance, because ethics naturally affect the democratic nature of institutions. The third type of definition, legalistic, allows laws and codes of ethical conduct to decide what is ethical and what is not. On the surface this definition is atheoretical. It does not require that unethical behaviors be harmful, but simply that a code or law states that certain behaviors are not allowed. Being stated in law does not mean the standards are beyond debate, although hopefully what the law deems unacceptable would be based on societal mores and a desire to improve the legislative process.

The operational definition used in this book best reflects the last definition: examining violations of codes and laws. To identify unethical behavior I use any official complaint that a member violated the House rules or law. However, throughout the book I explore the relationship between the codified ethical standards and the ability of Congress to fulfill its lawmaking and representational duties. Unethical behavior in a legislature, with most any definition, can lead to an illegitimate process and have negative consequences for a nation's policies. The absence of proper ethical judgment can have very real consequences that extend beyond the legislature's walls. Paolo Mauro's (1995, 1997) examination of economic growth in several countries and Donatella della Porta and Alberto Vannucci's (1997) examination of corruption in Italy found that corruption increased inefficiencies by giving resources to unprofitable businesses and by increasing the costs and distorting the demands for services. In addition, Friedman, Johnson, Kaufman, & Zoido-Lobaton (2000) examined sixty-nine countries and found that corruption led to businesses going underground, a smaller tax base, and smaller government. Comparative research has also found that corruption in governments is related to people evaluating the political system as less legitimate (Seligson, 2002) and less trustworthy, and give it less social capital (della Porta, 2000). Corruption has also been found to be related to lower levels of education funding (Mauro, 1997). In this country, Senators Alan Cranston (D, CA), Donald Reigle (D, MI), Dennis DeConcini (D, AZ), John Glenn (D, OH), and John McCain (R, AZ) were charged with improper influence on behalf of Charles Keating and the savings and loan industry. Investigators allege that the "Keating 5," as the senators were known, prevented federal regulators from taking proper action against Keating and his Lincoln Savings and Loan. The final price tag of the scandal cost U.S. taxpayers $2 billion (*Congressional Ethics: History, Facts, and Controversy*, 1992, p. 118).

A key reason unethical behaviors can lead to poor policies is because they can harm the legislative process. Dennis Thompson (1995) succinctly summed up this role when he observed that "when ethics are in disorder, or when citizens believe they are, disputes about ethics drive out discussion about public policies. . . . Ethics makes democracy safe for debate on the substance of public policy" (p. 18). In addition, ethical behavior should be valued by legislators because it assists them in maintaining the integrity of the process by meeting the legislative principles of independence, fairness, and accountability (Thompson, 1995). The Hastings Center (1985) identified similar principles but with different language: autonomy, accountability, and responsibility.

According to Thompson (1995) the legislative obligation of independent decision making requires that legislators make their decisions based on the merits of the policy under consideration. According to this principle, when evaluating policies, legislators may consider a variety of factors, such as the opinions of their constituents and the stated position of their political party.[7] Legislators are not, however, to be influenced by opinions and forces irrelevant to deliberations. The Hastings Center (1985) echoes this reasoning when it notes that decisions must be autonomous, meaning "legislators have an obligation to deliberate and decide, free from improper influence" (p. 34). Independence or autonomy is desired, since it increases the odds that decisions will be fair, legitimate, and made in the public's interest.

Legislative decisions in which the standard of independence is compromised weaken the deliberative process. Consider a legislator whose decision to support a policy is shaped by those who provided campaign funds during the most recent election, rather than the interests of his or her constituents. The result is that the contributors' interests carry unjustified influence, while the interests of those with legitimate claims to the legislator's efforts, such as constituents, are discounted. A further difficulty for the legislative process occurs when this decision process is revealed and attention shifts from the merits of the policy to the ethical appropriateness of the legislator's decision calculus. Instead of deliberating as to whether the decision benefits or hinders the collective constituency, the public's attention is diverted to the legislator's decision to consider his or her private interests. Constituents, unfortunately, conclude that their interests matter less than the private interests of the law-maker. Paul Heywood (1997) observes that this situation is particularly harmful for democracies: "The effects of corruption are especially disruptive in democracies: by attacking some of the basic principles on which democracy rests—notably, the equality of citizens before institutions (that is, the idea that individuals should be treated with fairness and respect by government offi-cials) and the openness of decision making (that is, crucially accountability)—corruption contributes to the delegitimation of the political and institutional systems in which it takes root" (p. 421).

These concerns are closely related to another of the legislative principles: accountability. Accountability requires that elected officials behave in a way that sustains public confidence (Thompson, 1995). Public confidence is nec-essary for democratic institutions, since their survival depends on citizen in-puts at a number of points, such as voting, paying taxes, supporting laws, and campaigning. Consequently, actions, actual or perceived, that diminish the public's confidence are harmful to the legislative process. A legislator who accepts money from a party interested in a particular legislative action may not be influenced by the gift. However, if the public *perceives* that the legisla-tor was influenced, then accepting the money would still be considered un-ethical, as it violates the public's trust. In short, this standard requires not only that legislative actions themselves be proper, but that legislators also be *per-ceived* as behaving ethically. The circumstances of the action become as im-portant as the action itself.

Third, the principle of fairness requires that members "fulfill their obliga-tions to colleagues, staff, challengers, other officials, and the institution as a whole" (Thompson, 1995, p. 22). Generally, members need to do their share of the work and play by the rules, and the rules need to be fair. Legislators have an obligation, according to this principle, to act and be treated fairly in their dealings with fellow legislators, constituents, and others. In addition, fairness involves members of a legislative institution having an obligation to-ward their colleagues and the body in which they serve. It is not fair if some members skirt their legislative responsibilities while others are workhorses.

The failure of members to uphold standards of fairness unquestionably dam-ages the reputation and integrity of the institution. Abuses that may seem mi-nor or even routine erode the public's confidence in the legislative function.

Abuses of the frank, special parking privileges at the airport, drawing small advances on future paychecks from the House bank, and other events have served to damage the reputation of the House and create the impression that the American political system is "fairer" to some than others. Integrity and reputation are sources of legitimacy and should be important to the public as well as high on the minds of legislators.

Taken together, these interrelated obligations require that legislators base their decisions on the merits of the proposal, that their dealings with others demonstrate concern for their colleagues and the reputation of the institution, and that they pay attention to the perception created by their actions. An institution that successfully meets each of these obligations would be one with the ability to focus on the business of legislation free from the distractions created by ethical lapses. Ideally, efforts to develop ethics standards would attempt to meet these obligations and focus on preventing errors in ethical judgment.

Another value of legislative ethics is they can insure that legislative resources are used for legislating. Many types of ethics violations divert valuable resources away from their primary purpose: lawmaking. Members who sexually harass their staff may not violate the legislative principles detailed here; however, their actions very likely prevent these employees from functioning at their highest level. Or members who are drunk at meetings may not violate the principles but are unlikely to be performing at their best. Similarly, members who use government resources for their personal use are necessarily diverting those resources away from important lawmaking and representative functions.

The ethics standards attempted to change the ethical behavior of House members. To the extent that they have addressed and affected behaviors harmful to the legislative process, the reforms can be considered at least a partial success. Chapter 2 focuses on this issue, but although several investigations note that problems with members' ethical behaviors remain, most acknowledge that the House is cleaner today than it has been in the past (Baker, 1985; Garment, 1991, introduction; Harris, 1995, chap. 2; Thompson, 1995, introduction; but see Sabato & Simpson, 1996). Because rules and guidelines for ethical behavior are clearer and more precise, and because the media are willing to exploit scandals, members appear less likely to display the blatant unethical behaviors that were once more common. For example, it has been estimated that in the 1830s as many as 25 percent of Congress's members received unsecured loans from the Bank of the United States during debates on rechartering the bank (Baker, 1985, p. 8). Or, more recently, many of the ethical lapses that cost members such as Jim Wright or Dan Rostenkowski their careers were permitted when they entered Congress.

While the ethics standards to date may have had positive effects on members' behavior, they still may not be cost beneficial. There are unintended consequences of almost any reform (Rieselbach, 1994). As with other reforms, existing ethics reforms likely had unintended effects that harmed the legislative process. One potential negative effect is harming the accountability principle. The reforms have brought to light behaviors that previously went unnoticed, thereby tarnishing the public's perception of Congress. Prior to codifying standards of behavior and efforts to monitor members' actions, unethical behaviors went largely undetected and unreported because, quite simply, there were few rules to violate. The advent of institutional rules related to ethical behavior provided a cache of information about unethical behavior and has perhaps contributed to Americans' low regard for Congress. In short, rules that were intended to render members more ethical may actually damage the perception many have of the legislative branch.

The increased attention to ethical behavior may also cause Congress to divert attention from its legislative and representative obligations. This diversion is likely felt most by members of the ethics committees. Members serving on the Committee of Standards of Official Conduct are not serving the direct interests of their constituents, nor are they making public law when they investigate their colleagues. This has made service on this committee very unattractive to members. According to Ann McBride, Representative Steve Schiff (R, NM), former member of the committee, stated that service on the ethics committee is so burdensome that "it may be we're going to have to get Members intoxicated to get them to serve on the ethics Committee" (U.S. House, 1997, 75). In fact, in 1997 the House adopted procedural reforms for the ethics process that minimize the costs to the committee membership.[8] Floor time for legislating may also be lost. When considering sanctions against a member, the full chamber may spend several hours debating the issue. When the House voted recently to expel Traficant, it spent three hours debating his fate on the eve of recess, when members needed to deal with legislation. When leaders are involved in scandals, more time and energy is diverted away from legislating. Leaders have obligations to their parties and to the institution, yet when they are focused on their own ethical problems their ability to lead may be weakened. Ethical issues revolving around leaders draw more media and public attention and reflect more broadly on the institution as a whole. Consider the plight of Speaker Newt Gingrich, the House Republicans, and the 105th session of Congress. Amid charges of ethical wrongdoing, Speaker Gingrich was subjected to intense public scrutiny. His ability to lead was questioned as some in his own party called for him to step aside until the issue was resolved. Instead of boldly leading the Congress with firebrand furor as he did during the 104th Congress, the Speaker instead presided over a more divided party and was less able to pass significant pieces of legislation. About the only major action taken in 1997 was to reprimand Speaker Gingrich. Simply put, Speaker Gingrich's inability to lead the 105th Congress in the same manner as he did the early days of the 104th was, in part, caused by his ethical problem (Koszczuk, 1997; Koszczuk & Weisman, 1997).

Problems arise even when nonleaders are accused. When members who have ethical problems are expelled or encouraged to resign during a term, voters are denied the representative they voluntarily elected.[9] Although expelled members are likely to lose some support from voters, the effects may be surprisingly small. Representative Michael Myers, who was expelled for his involvement in Abscam (see the Glossary of Key Scandals for more detail), ran for reelection and received his party's nomination even after his expulsion. Furthermore, after a member is expelled the district lacks representation until the next election. Following Rep. Traficant's recent expulsion, the House allowed some of his staff to stay on to deal with constituents' requests for casework so that the constituents would still get at least some benefits, even if they had no voice during policy considerations. If a member resigns to avoid questions of ethics, there can also be a delay between the resignation and the seating of the new member. Such a loss in representation may come during a period of critical importance to the district. Even members who remain in office during ethics investigations may be distracted by the allegations to the point that they focus mainly on defending themselves instead of representing their district. Members may miss votes, for example, to attend meetings with lawyers or attend their trial. Any time members spend defending themselves is time diverted from the important tasks of representing their districts and making policy. This not only is a loss of members' time but also relates to the fairness principle. Members not fully engaged are not fulfilling their obligations to the institution. Even members who have not been accused or involved in the investigations may lose time. Alan Rosenthal (1996) made this point in the context of state legislators who have devoted increased attention to ethical issues when he observed that "with the stakes so high, the attention of legislators is diverted from trying to solve the problems of the state to protecting themselves from possible (and inadvertent) wrongdoing" (p. 214).

Ethics investigations also can make legislation difficult when they are used for political purposes. This use of ethics is likely to increase acrimony and partisanship in the chamber, decreasing the ability of Congress to pass legislation. As noted earlier, Ginsberg and Shefter (1990) suggest that as electoral politics weakened during the 1970s they were replaced with institutional politics, which involve fights for power within the institutional context instead of the electoral context. One of the components of institutional politics is the use of scandal to embarrass and weaken opponents. Suzanne Garment (1991, chap. 2) suggests that bringing ethics charges is like a boomerang. After members of one party have been accused, the accused party is apt to bring retaliatory charges against the other. She sees the Congressional scandals following Watergate in this light. The executive branch and Republicans may have pursued Abscam in retaliation for Congress's investigations of President Richard Nixon. Similarly, many Republicans see the charges against Newt Gingrich as a tit-for-tat action for the toppling of Democratic Speaker Jim Wright. The Conservative Opportunity Society serves to demonstrate the political use of ethics. Gingrich and other Republican House members created the society to build up the Republican Party, in part, by investigating and bringing charges against House

Democrats. The use of the ethics procedures for political purposes harms not only the legislative and democratic processes by wasting resources on unjustified charges, but also serves to increase conflict in the chamber and undermine the public's confidence in the institution.[10]

Yet another potential and unintended consequence of the heightened concern with ethics is a decrease in the number and quality of people willing to serve in Congress. By increasing the costs and decreasing the benefits of Congressional service, the reforms made it less rational for individuals to desire to be in Congress.[11] Today's candidates must learn the ethics standards and legal requirements to run for office. Once elected, officials must learn additional ethics standards for holding office, and hire attorneys. To make the situation more costly, Congress, in recent years, has removed many of the perks that made Congressional service attractive. Members have lost many opportunities to earn outside incomes, while gifts, trips, and honoraria for personal use have been limited. Finally, if a member is accused of a violation, whether correctly or not, it is costly to his or her personal, financial, and political lives. Legal costs can run in the hundreds of thousands of dollars, reputations can be destroyed, members' children may have problems at school, and the media can hound their spouses (Garment, 1991, chap. 10).[12] If the member is guilty of severe wrongdoing, the costs may be justified; however, if the member is innocent, the personal costs are not warranted. Potential members who observe legislators damaged by charges are less likely to seek Congressional service and its accompanying intense public scrutiny. Rosenthal (1996) noted that the hostile climate in state legislatures caused by ethics investigations has resulted in "some of the ablest legislators" retiring because they "no longer have the stomach for what they must endure" (p. 14).

THE REMAINDER OF THE BOOK

The remainder of the book examines the effects of the ethics climate and subsequent reforms: What effect did they have on members' ethical behaviors? What effect did they have on the ability of the House to legislate? What have been the unintended consequences? The thesis is this: When the ethics climate unearthed ethical misconduct, investigated and publicized the misconduct, it created some nagative consequences for the House. However, these costs were relatively small compared to the improvements in members' behavior resulting from the ethics climate.

Chapter 2 provides background information on the development of ethics standards in the House and outlines changes in ethics standards over time. This chapter also examines the behaviors addressed in the reforms to see if the reforms have improved the legislative process. Evidence from a survey of former members suggests that since the 1970s House members have altered their behavior to comply with the rules. It also suggests that the ethics reforms have decreased behaviors that potentially harm the legislative process. For information on the different ethics violations, Appendix A lists all of the accusations made against members from 1977 to 2000, and there is a Glossary of Key Scandals. This glossary briefly outlines many cases of unethical behavior discussed in the book.

In addition to improving members' ethics, another goal of the reforms was to improve the public's confidence in Congress. Chapter 3 examines how the ethics climate and reforms have affected the public's approval of Congress. When accounts of members' unethical behaviors were reported in the press the overall approval ratings fell modestly. It takes several newspaper stories for changes in the public's approval of Congress to be noticeable, but sometimes there are numerous stories. The chapter also finds that Congress can recoup some of its lost esteem by disciplining a member. When Congress disciplined a member the approval ratings rose. In addition, concern over ethics in the Congress harms the approval of the membership more than Congress the institution. Thus, the conclusion of Chapter 3 is that while the reforms may not have increased Congressional approval, they have not significantly harmed the public's support of Congress.

Besides changing members' behavior, another way the ethics climate and reforms could improve the ethics in the chamber is by removing members who violate the ethics standards. Chapter 4 provides evidence that members who were accused and convicted of violating the ethics standards were likely to leave Congress within two election cycles, but a lack of electoral competition in districts and members' power in the chamber can minimize the chances that members leave. The chapter also discusses a potential negative effects of the reforms: encouraging members who have not violated the standards to leave. Using a survey of former members, evidence is provided suggesting that the reforms have increased the costs and decreased the benefits of service and may have caused some early retirements.

Chapter 5 explores another potential side effect of the standards: harming the ability of Congress to pass legislation. By examining whether investigations of members' ethics affected the number of bills and major bills passed by Congress, it is concluded that the investigations had a modest negative effect on the total number of bills, but not the number of major bills passed. This chapter also examines the ability of members who have been accused of violating the ethics rules to carry out their responsibilities, concluding that the largest effect that the standards have had on legislating is limiting the ability of those accused to carry out their responsibilities.

Chapter 6 takes a slight turn and tries to explain which members were likely to be accused and convicted of violating the ethics standards. It uses a fairly simple model to predict that members with the opportunity to violate standards (have leadership positions, or are in the majority party), the propensity or desire to do so (are less wealthy, but strong party supporters), and who perceive fewer costs to violating the standards (have less political ambition, less well-educated voters, and win reelections easily) were more likely to violate the standards than other members. This is examined to discover ways to further limit unethical behaviors and identify potential biases in the ethics process.

The concluding chapter summarizes the previous chapters and offers three recommendations to improve the ethics process. The suggestions are designed to minimize the negative effects of the reforms while improving the ethical behavior of members. First, the recruitment and election of candidates need to insure that ethical citizens are elected to office, since violations are costly to the legislative process. Second, the system of investigation should include procedures that minimize costs and increase the fairness of investigative inquiries. Instead of relying solely on self-discipline, an outside commission whose duty is to investigate charges of unethical behavior and make disciplinary recommendations should be created. Such a commission should minimize some of the partisanship and bias that exists in investigations, since members will not be passing judgment on each other or their leaders. Finally, a procedure to discourage false or frivolous charges against members should be developed. The investigations of members harm the legislative principles of fairness and accountability and deplete legislative resources. Thus, charges that are purely politically motivated must be prevented. To accomplish this, Congress should consider disciplining members who bring such charges.

NOTES

1. The Iran Contra scandal involved U.S. officials selling arms to Iran, a nation the United States had hostile relations with, in order to give aid to the Nicaraguan Contras, a rebel group fighting the Sandinsta government, in violation of U.S. law.

2. Richard Nixon resigned because of the role he played in the Watergate scandal. Spiro Agnew resigned because of Internal Revenue Service charges that he failed to pay his taxes.

3. While Judicial Watch is suing Cheney because of the accounting practices of Halliburton while he was CEO, the Security and Exchange Commission is also investigating the business practices of the corporation. President George W. Bush's previous business dealings also have been investigated and brought out during the corporate scandals of 2002, but appear less likely to lead to civil or criminal problems.

4. For example, Hazel O'Leary, who served as secretary of energy, resigned amidst criticism of her lavish tax-paid trips and was accused of illegal campaign financing (Schmidt, 1997). Also during the Clinton presidency, the secretary of agriculture, Mike Espy, resigned to fight criminal charges of corruption (Neal, 1998). In the long run, neither O'Leary nor Espy was convicted of any wrongdoing.

5. For example, John Tower, President George H. Bush's nominee for secretary of defense, faced charges of womanizing and being a heavy drinker, while Zoe Baird, President Clinton's choice for attorney general, withdrew her nomination because she failed to pay Social Security taxes for illegal immigrants in her employ.

6. The House and the Senate started to develop a code of conduct for themselves and an infrastructure to enforce the code during the 1960s. Thus, the beginnings of the ethics climate predates Watergate. However, it is clear that by the time President Richard Nixon resigned the ethics climate was thriving.

7. A problem for legislators is knowing whose opinion or interests should be used to evaluate the merits. One way to think of this problem is to ask if members should act like trustees following their own judgment or delegates following their constituents' judgments. It is similarly difficult to identify members' constituents. Is it the nation, or the district? If the district, should any consideration be made for those who vote or otherwise support you?

8. These reforms include allowing members not on the committee to serve on subcommittees created for specific cases.

9. In addition, the House is one member short, thereby marginally increasing the workload of other members and harming the fairness principle.

10. Along similar lines, investigations of scandals divert Americans' attention from the real issues of fitness for office. By establishing rules and laws to limit politicians' behavior, Americans defer to the law and to lawyers about what is acceptable behavior for politicians. Issues of fitness for office become whether a law was technically broken, rather than whether the politician is serving the nation well. In reference to the scandals surrounding President Clinton, Robert F. Bauer (1998) said:

The expectations, that the scandal will turn on the resolution of legal issues, needs to be challenged. Somehow the Starr investigation has come to be seen as the functional equivalent of an impeachment process; should he conclude that laws were broken, the question of the President's fitness to hold office will have effectively been settled. This is a dangerous view. . . . The Constitution does not envision that any and all charges alleging violations of law will serve as a basis for impeachment, The Founders had in mind political crimes. (p. 9)

11. The literature on Congressional emergence and retirement both suggest that members and potential candidates make rational calculations (see, for example, Williams & Lascher, 1993).

12. Charges of wrongdoing can be expensive for members. Newt Gingrich spent about $700,000 in legal representation to fight allegations of unethical behavior (Gettinger, 1998, p. 1194). In 2002, Sen. Torricelli spent over $3 million in lawyer fees (Kane, 2002). Thus, since the 1980s, Congress has allowed members to raise funds in order to pay for legal costs incurred as a result of their legislative service. Raising the large sums of money needed for legal defense takes members away from their legislative work. It can also increase the appearance of wrongdoing on the part of the member. During debates on health care reform, Rep. Daniel Rostenkowski, chair of the Ways and Means Committee, accepted money for his legal defense fund from insurance companies and others with vested interests in health care (Clark, 1997).

Chapter 2

Improvements in Congressional Ethics

In 1798, Representatives Matthew Lyon and Roger Griswold brawled on the House floor after Lyon spat at Griswold for saying disparaging words about his lack of a distinguished military career. In the same year, Senator William Blount incited two Native American tribes to attack Spanish Florida and Louisiana. During the debates over slavery, Representative Preston Brooks bludgeoned Senator Charles Sumner with a cane so severely that he did not return to the Congress for three years. A few years earlier, Senator Harry Foote, someone prone to duel, threatened Senator Thomas Hart Benton of Missouri with a pistol and had to be restrained by his colleagues. Daniel Webster demanded a retainer to represent the interests of the Bank of the United States on Capitol Hill. In the early Congresses, members frequently carried knives and firearms, the floor was littered with spittoons, and some members occasionally brought their dogs to the chamber.

Congress today is more orderly and has a tougher code of ethics than the description of the Congress offered here. The legislative career of Rep. Dan Rostenkowski (D, IL) was, in many ways, emblematic of the changing nature of ethics in the U.S. House. In 1994, Rep. Rostenkowski, then chairman of the House Ways and Means Committee, was indicted on seventeen felony counts of embezzlement and fraud. He was accused of having ghost employees, converting stamps bought with government funds into cash, and using taxpayer monies and campaign funds to buy cars, personal items, and gifts. Eventually Rostenkowski pled guilty to two felonies and was sentenced to seventeen months in jail. Perhaps ironically, Rostenkowski was first elected to Congress in 1958, the year the initial government code of ethics was enacted. While in Congress, Rostenkowski developed a style that took advantage of the perks of office. Over the course of his many years in Congress, the House's ethics standards for members' behavior became tougher; however, Rostenkowski's practices did not evolve to accommodate the changing criteria. In 1994, Rep. Robert Torricelli (D, NJ) aptly noted that Rostenkowski did not change with the times when he observed, "He is being prosecuted for things which, a generation ago, were probably somewhat accepted" (Hook, 1994, p. 1360).[1]

To demonstrate the growing concern with appropriate behavior, this chapter charts the history of ethics guidelines in the House. In addition, it describes the development of the ethics standards and evaluates their effect on the legislative process and members' behaviors.

ETHICS PRIOR TO 1958

The early Congresses had very few guidelines to instruct members as to what constituted appropriate or inappropriate behavior. The U.S. Constitution is notoriously brief and vague, and it keeps to this trend regarding Congressional ethics. The Constitution establishes minimal qualifications for holding office, such as age, citizenship, and residency requirements, but is largely silent on what should comprise grounds for discipline. It is also silent about which punishments should be levied for unethical behaviors, other than to say that "each House may determine the Rules of its Proceedings, punish its Members for disorderly Behaviour, and, with the Concurrence of two thirds, expel a Member" (Article I, Section 5).

Although the House waited until the last half of the twentieth century to develop a formal code of conduct, some laws limited behaviors, and it did occasionally take action against members prior to this. An examination of both early and recent disciplinary actions provides an indication of what the House has historically considered inappropriate behavior. Table 2.1 lists each expulsion proceeding in the House, Table 2.2 each censure proceeding, and Table 2.3 each reprimand. One thing to note initially is that the proceedings often fail, and often after one proceeding failed, a lighter action was attempted. Prior to 1958 only three out of twenty-nine expulsion attempts were successful. Of these twenty-six failed attempts, eleven also had censure votes, eight of which were successful. Of the thirty censure attempts, twelve failed. In addition, prior to 1958 the bulk of the ethics cases did not involve corruption as we think of it today, but rather attacks (either verbal or physical) on other members or offensive utterances on the part of a member. Around the time of the Civil War, a few cases dealt with charges of treason and corruption. The corruption cases were related to an Iowa loan, the Credit Mobilier case, and "selling appointments to the military academies" (Baker, 1985, p. 12).

In the early House, decisions to sanction members for ethical lapses were dealt with on a case-by-case basis and relied primarily on societal norms of decency (Baker, 1985, pp. 3–4). In the absence of clear ethics guidelines, decisions to discipline members were based on informal norms and lacked consistency. Actions that today clearly violate the ethics standards were permissible in earlier periods, while today's acceptable behaviors were sometimes sanctioned. For example, bribery, which is clearly unacceptable today, was to some degree tolerated until 1853, when laws against it were enacted. In the 1830s it was estimated that as many as 25 percent of Congress's members received unsecured loans from the Bank of the United States during debates on rechartering the bank (Baker, 1985, p. 8). As a stark contrast, in 1832, while bribery was being ignored, Representative William Stanbery (JD, OH) was censured for merely suggesting that "the eyes of the Speaker were too frequently turned from the chair you occupy toward the White House" (*Congressional Ethics*, 1980, p. 14). The obvious inconsistency in disciplining members continued six years later when Representatives William J. Graves (W, KY) and Henry Wise (TD, VA) went unpunished for killing a fellow member during a duel.

Another inconsistency in the handling of ethics is the absence of disciplinary cases in the mid-twentieth century (see Tables 2.1 through 2.3). It is hard to imagine that this period was entirely void of ethical missteps. In fact, there were several scandals during this time, such as Rep. Wilber Mills's (D, AR) relationship with a stripper named Fanne Foxe or Rep. Adam Clayton Powell's (D, NY) exclusion. Instead, the absence of disciplinary cases was most likely caused by the Great Depression, World War II, Vietnam, and the Civil Rights movement occupying Congress's and the country's time and energy. Given the weighty nature of these issues, it is not surprising that Congress devoted less attention to the appropriateness of members' behavior, even though it overlaps the beginning of the ethics climate.

Partisanship is another characteristic of the early House's enforcement of ethics standards (Getz, 1966, pp. 98–112; Thompson, 1995, pp. 146–150). Getz (1966, p. 100) notes that party-line voting occurred on "frequent occasions." He found evidence of partisanship in the four cases he examined in the House; Rep. B. P. Whittemore's (R, SC) remittance to the House and the censureship of Reps. Oakes Ames (R, MA), James Brooks (D, NY), and William Kelley (R, PA). Getz observes that the emotionally charged nature of ethics proceedings provides a "fertile culture in which partisan sentiments can blur calm legislative judgment" (p. 102).

Several explanations may be offered for Congress's inconsistent enforcement of ethics standards during its first 150 years. One reason is that the nature of the Congressional environment did not readily lend itself to a tough ethics code. Partisan politics and the "club spirit" are frequently cited as reasons that Congress has been reluctant to discipline its members. Members rely on each other and see their fellow members as part of a team, and therefore do not wish to make enemies of those whom they might need to rely on at a later date. According to former Speaker Champ Clark, "Men who fight together in this legislative body have a feeling approximating that of the soldiers' feeling for one another" (Wilson, 1951, p. 222). This notion of esprit de corps also helps explain why members did not favor formal ethics rules (Wilson, 1951). When formal rules are in place it is typically clear when a rule has been vio-

Table 2.1
Cases of Expulsion in the House

Congress	Session	Year	Member	Grounds	Disposition
5th	2nd	1798	Matthew Lyon, Anti-Fed.—Vt.	Assault on representative	Not expelled
5th	2nd	1798	Roger Griswold, Fed.—Conn.	Assault on representative	Not expelled
5th	3rd	1799	Matthew Lyon, Anti-Fed.—Vt.	Sedition	Not expelled
25th	2nd	1838	William J. Graves, Whig—Ky.	Killing of representative in a duel	Not expelled
25th	3rd	1839	Alexander Duncan, Whig—Ohio	Offensive publication	Not expelled
34th	1st	1856	Preston S. Brooks, State Rights Dem.—S.C.	Assault on senator	Not expelled
34th	3rd	1857	Orsamus B. Matteson, Whig—N.Y.	Corruption	Not expelled
34th	3rd	1857	William Gilbert, Whig—N.Y.	Corruption	Not expelled
34th	3rd	1857	William Welch, American—Conn.	Corruption	Not expelled
34th	3rd	1857	Francis S. Edwards, American—N.Y.	Corruption	Not expelled
35th	1st	1858	Orsamus B. Matteson, Whig—N.Y.	Corruption	Not expelled
37th	1st	1861	John B. Clark, D—Mo.	Support of rebellion	Expelled
37th	1st	1861	Henry C. Burnett, D—Ky.	Support of rebellion	Expelled
37th	1st	1861	John W. Reid, D—Mo.	Support of rebellion	Expelled
38th	1st	1864	Alexader Long, D—Ohio	Treasonable utterance	Not expelled*
38th	1st	1864	Benjamin G. Harris, D—MD	Treasonable utterance	Not expelled*

Table 2.1 (*continued*)

Congress	Session	Year	Member	Grounds	Disposition
39th	1st	1866	Lovell H. Rousseau, R—Ky.	Assault on representative	Not expelled*
41st	2nd	1870	Benjamin Whittemore, R—S.C.	Corruption	Not expelled*
41st	2nd	1870	Roderick R. Butler, R—Tenn.	Corruption	Not expelled*
42nd	3rd	1873	Oakes Ames, R—Mass.	Corruption	Not expelled*
42nd	3rd	1873	James Brooks, D—N.Y.	Corruption	Not expelled*
43rd	2nd	1875	John Y. Brown, D—Ky.	Insult to representative	Not expelled*
44th	1st	1875	William S. King, R—Minn.	Corruption	Not expelled
44th	1st	1875	John G. Shumaker, D—N.Y.	Corruption	Not expelled
48th	1st	1884	William P. Kellogg, R—La.	Corruption	Not expelled
67th	1st	1921	Thomas L. Blanton, D—Texas	Abuse of leave to print	Not expelled*
96th	1st	1979	Charles C. Diggs Jr., D—Mich.	Misuse of clerk-hire funds	Not expelled*
96th	2nd	1980	Michael J. Myers, D—Pa.	Corruption	Expelled
107th	2nd	2002	James Traficant, D—Ohio	Corruption	Expelled†

Source: Congressional Ethics: History, Facts, and Controversy (Washington, D.C.: Congressional Quarterly Press, 1992), 167.

*Censured after expulsion move failed or was withdrawn.

†Not in *Congressional Ethics*, 1992.

Table 2.2
Censure Proceedings in the House

Congress	Session	Year	Member	Grounds	Disposition
5th	2nd	1798	Matthew Lyon, Anti-Fed.—Vt.	Assault on representative	Not censured
5th	2nd	1798	Roger Griswold, Fed.—Conn.	Assault on representative	Not censured
22nd	1st	1832	William Stanbery, J.D.—Ohio	Insult to Speaker	Censured
24th	1st	1836	Sherrod Williams, Whig—Ky.	Insult to Speaker	Not censured
25th	2nd	1838	Henry A. Wise, Tyler Dem.—Va.	Serve as second in duel	Not censured
25th	3rd	1839	Alexander Duncan, Whig—Ohio	Offensive publication	Not censured
27th	2nd	1842	John Q. Adams, Whig—Mass.	Treasonable petition	Not censured
27th	2nd	1842	Joshua R. Giddings, Whig—Ohio	Offensive paper	Censured
34th	2nd	1856	Henry Edmundson, D—Va.	Complicity in assault on senator	Not censured
34th	2nd	1856	Laurence M. Keitt, D—S.C.	Complicity in assault on senator	Censured
36th	1st	1860	George S. Houston, D—Ala.	Insult to representative	Not censured
38th	1st	1864	Alexander Long, D—Ohio	Treasonable utterance	Censured
38th	1st	1864	Benjamin G. Harris, D—Md.	Treasonable utterance	Censured
39th	1st	1866	John W. Chanler, D—N.Y.	Insult to House	Censured
39th	1st	1866	Lovell H. Rousseau, R—Ky.	Assault to representative	Censured
40th	1st	1867	John W. Hunter, Ind—N.Y.	Insult to representative	Censured
40th	2nd	1868	Fernando Wood, D—N.Y.	Offensive utterance	Censured
40th	3rd	1868	E. D. Holbrook, D—Idaho	Offensive utterance	Censured[1]
41st	2nd	1870	Benjamin F. Whittemore, R—S.C.	Corruption	Censured
41st	2nd	1870	Roderick R. Butler, R—Tenn.	Corruption	Censured

Table 2.2 (*continued*)

Congress	Session	Year	Member	Grounds	Disposition
41st	2nd	1870	John T. Deweese, D—N.C.	Corruption	Censured
42nd	3rd	1873	Oakes Ames, R—Mass.	Corruption	Censured
42nd	3rd	1873	James Brooks, D—N.Y.	Corruption	Censured
43rd	2nd	1875	John Y. Brown, D—Ky.	Insult to representative	Censured[2]
44th	1st	1876	James G. Blaine, R—Maine	Corruption	Not censured
47th	1st	1882	William D. Kelley, R—Pa.	Offensive utterance	Not censured
47th	1st	1882	John D. White, R—Ky.	Offensive utterance	Not censured
47th	2nd	1883	John Van Voorhis, R—N.Y.	Offensive utterance	Not censured
51st	1st	1890	William D. Bynum, D—Ind.	Offensive utterance	Censured
67th	1st	1921	Thomas L. Blanton, D—Texas	Abuse of leave to print	Censured
95th	2nd	1978	Edward Roybal, D—Calif.	Lying to House committee	Not censured[3]
96th	1st	1979	Charles C. Diggs Jr., D—Mich.	Misuse of clerk-hire funds	Censured
96th	2nd	1980	Charles H. Wilson, D—Calif.	Financial misconduct	Censured
98th	1st	1983	Gerry E. Studds, D—Mass.	Sexual misconduct	Censured
98th	1st	1983	Daniel B. Crane, R—Ill.	Sexual misconduct	Censured
101st	2nd	1990	Barney Frank, D—Mass.	Discrediting House	Not censured[3]

Source: Congressional Ethics: History, Facts, and Controversy (Washington, D.C.: Congressional Quarterly Press, 1992), 171–172.

1. Holbrook was a territorial delegate, not a representative.
2. The House later rescinded part of the censure resolution against Brown.
3. Reprimanded after censure resolution failed or was withdrawn.

Table 2.3
Reprimand Proceedings in the House

Congress	Session	Year	Member	Grounds	Disposition
94th	2nd	1976	Robert L. F. Sikes, D—Fla.	Financial misconduct	Reprimanded
95th	2nd	1978	John J. McFall, D—Calif.	Financial misconduct	Reprimanded
95th	2nd	1978	Edward Roybal, D—Calif.	Financial misconduct	Reprimanded
95th	2nd	1978	Charles H. Wilson, D—Calif.	Financial misconduct	Reprimanded
98th	2nd	1984	George V. Hansen, R—Idaho	Financial misconduct	Reprimanded
100th	1st	1987	Austin J. Murphy, D—Pa.	Misuse of office	Reprimanded
101st	2nd	1990	Barney Frank, D—Mass.	Discrediting House	Reprimanded
105th	1st	1997	Newt Gingrich, R—Ga.	Discrediting House	Reprimanded*

Source: Congressional Ethics: History, Facts, and Controversy (Washington, D.C.: Congressional Quarterly Press, 1992), 172.

*Not in *Congressional Ethics*, 1992.

lated; the members are then placed in a position where they have little option except to vote against friends.

A second set of explanations for the inconsistent application of the ethics standards is philosophically based. Some have argued that the ethics of the House should replicate society's mores, and that in an individualistic society, individuals both in and out of politics are afforded great leeway in ethical matters (Wilson, 1951, p. 227).[2] Consequently, charges of ethics lapses should be evaluated in a flexible manner and without the hindrance of strict rules. In addition, some believe that if anyone is to evaluate alleged ethics lapses, it should be the voters who are called on to pass judgment on members' behaviors. It has been argued that voters are capable of evaluating the appropriateness of members' behaviors, and that they have a right to elect whomever they please to represent them, regardless of what others think about the member.

A third reason for the inconsistent application of ethics standards, particularly in the formative years of the Congress, is that it frequently takes considerable time for institutions to develop appropriate and widely accepted standards of conduct. Nelson Polsby (1968), in formulating his theory of institutionalization, contends that some characteristics that distinguish institutions such as the U.S. House of Representatives from other organizations are the application and emergence of universalistic rules and the rise of professionalism. Consequently, one reason that appropriate ethics standards were lacking in the early years of the Congress is that the institution simply was not developed enough to have settled on universally acceptable rules. Indeed, early efforts to discipline members lacked reliance on precedents and were frequently decided in an ad hoc and inconsistent fashion. Over the years, Congress came to terms with what offenses were punishable and whether offenses committed prior to the current Congress should be punished. In addition, the move to professionalize Congress brought with it, as has been the case in most professions, a recognition of the need for acceptable standards of conduct.

THE DEVELOPMENT OF ETHICS STANDARDS:
1958 AND BEYOND

The first effort to provide ethics guidelines for members came in 1958, when Congress passed codes of ethics for government employees, including House members. Although the codes were an important first step, they were quite weak and lacked any enforcement machinery. The codes stipulated that government employees, including members, be loyal to the government, uphold the Constitution, and work a full day for a full day's pay. They also encouraged whistle blowing on corruption and prohibited the dispensing of favors unfairly, among other things.

The following is the code of ethics for government service of 1958 (see http://www.house.gov/ethics):

1. Put loyalty to the highest moral principles and to country above loyalty to persons, party, or Government department.

2. Uphold the Constitution, laws and legal regulations of the United States and of all Governments therein, and never be a party to their evasion.

3. Give a full day's labor for a full day's pay; giving to the performance of his duties his earnest effort and best thought.

4. Seek to find and employ more efficient and economical ways of getting tasks accomplished.

5. Never discriminate unfairly by dispensing of special favors or privileges to anyone, whether for remuneration or not; and never accept, for himself or his family, favors or benefits under circumstances which might be construed by reasonable persons as influencing the performance of his governmental duties.

6. Make no private promises of any kind binding upon the duties of office, since a Government employee has no private word which can be binding on public duty.

7. Engage in no business with the Government, either directly or indirectly which is inconsistent with the conscientious performance of his governmental duties.

8. Never use any information coming to him confidentially in the performance of his governmental duties as a means of making private profit.

9. Expose corruption wherever discovered.

10. Uphold these principles, ever conscious that public office is a public trust.

The codes did not, however, contain enforcement provisions and did not suggest punishment for violations of the standards. Given the vague nature of the standards and the lack of meaningful enforcement mechanisms, few charges were actually levied against members.

It is difficult to determine whether the 1958 standards were the result of a preexisting ethics climate or whether the standards mark the embryonic stages of that climate. It is quite possible that the events of the 1950s served to create the ethics climate. Not only did the 1950s witness the investigations that led to the code of conduct, this period ushered McCarthyism to the forefront of social and political life.[3] Sen. Joe McCarthy (R, WI) used allegations of communism to attack political enemies and build his own reputation. More significantly, these attacks became institutionalized in the Committee on UnAmerican Activities, and this committee's allegations of wrongdoing against individuals ruined many reputations and destroyed professional and personal lives. The aftermath of these destructive activities may have taught those in Congress the value of politics by other means.

While the 1950s may properly be seen as the dawn of the ethics climate, it was not until the late 1960s and early 1970s that serious efforts to monitor legislative behavior occurred. Not surprisingly, the effort to develop a stronger code of conduct and an enforcement infrastructure followed a number of scandals. Three of the key scandals of the 1960s were Rep. Adam Clayton Powell's

(D, NY) exclusion, Sen. Thomas Dodd's (D, CT) censure, and the investigation of Bobby Baker. Baker had been secretary of the Senate and became a millionaire on his $19,000 a year job (*Congressional Ethics*, 1980, p. 91). In response to the events, the House created a select Committee on Standards of Official Conduct in 1967 to develop a new code. The following year a new code of ethical conduct was adopted. One by-product of the code was to create a permanent bipartisan Committee on Standards of Official Conduct to investigate accusations of unethical behavior. The code also prevented members from accepting large gifts from actors with a direct interest in legislation, limited honoraria to the "usual and customary" amount, prevented personal use of campaign funds except for reimbursements for campaign expenses, and prevented paying staff members if they did not work. Members were also required to disclose interest of more than $5,000, income of $1,000 or more in businesses working with the government, and sources of income or capital gain greater than $5,000. These disclosure rules were amended in 1970 to include honoraria of more than $300 or debts greater than $10,000.

Scandals would once again cause the House to revisit its treatment of ethical issues in the 1970s. Following Watergate and a number of House scandals, the House created the Obey Commission to develop a new code of ethics.[4] The House passed the bulk of the Obey report and made a few additional changes over the next few of years. By the time the decade ended, House members were limited in outside earnings, honoraria, receiving gifts from lobbyists, and in their ability to use the franking privilege. Members were required to disclose gifts, income, financial holdings, debts, real estate transactions, securities, and commodity transactions. The practice of transferring gifts to House accounts was also halted. All in all, the House had made considerable progress in formalizing the ethics standards.

Another reform that coincided with the code of conduct was the 1974 campaign finance law. Although portions of the law were eventually declared unconstitutional in *Buckley v. Valeo* (1976), the law served to limit members' behaviors and contributed to the growing body of ethics standards. Primarily, the law placed limits on the amount of money candidates could accept from donors and required the disclosure of campaign contributors. In 2002, Congress passed an additional campaign finance law. Interestingly, though, it did very little to limit what members or candidates could do; rather, it raised the amount of money they could raise from individual donors and limited parties' ability to raise soft money and outside groups' use of issue advocacy advertising.[5]

The 1977 ethics codes were the most stringent set of rules on members' behavior to date. Nevertheless, they still had numerous loopholes. Moreover, the Committee on Standards of Official Conduct rarely brought charges until after criminal investigations started, which served to undermine the notion that the House could police itself. Following what now appears to be an established pattern, Congress once again reacted to charges of ethics violations—

this time the cloud surrounding Speaker Jim Wright—by passing the Ethics Reform Act (1989). The act's main reforms included further limits on honoraria and outside income, as well as efforts to close the revolving door and prevent members from pocketing leftover campaign donations.[6] In addition, it expanded the House ethics committee's membership and responsibilities. The only substantive rule additions came in 1995, when Congress passed a tougher gift ban law. The following is the current code; see http://www.house.gov/ethics):[7]

1. A Member, officer, or employee of the House of Representatives shall conduct himself at all times in a manner that shall reflect creditably on the House of Representatives.

2. A Member, officer, or employee of the House of Representatives shall adhere to the spirit and the letter of the Rules of the House of Representatives and to the rules of duly constituted committees thereof.

3. A Member, officer, or employee of the House of Representatives shall receive no compensation nor shall he permit any compensation to accrue to his beneficial interest from any source, the receipt of which would occur by virtue of influence improperly exerted from his position in Congress.

4. A Member, officer, or employee of the House of Representatives shall not accept gifts (other than personal hospitality of an individual or with a fair market value of $100 or less) in any calendar year aggregation more than $250, directly or indirectly, from any person (other than from a relative) except to the extent permitted by written waiver granted in exceptional circumstances by the Committee on Standards of Official Conduct pursuant to clause 4(e) (1) (E) of rule X.

5. A Member, officer, or employee of the House of Representatives, shall accept no honorarium for a speech, writing for publication, or other similar activity.

6. A Member of the House of Representatives shall keep his campaign funds separate from his personal funds. A Member shall convert no campaign funds to personal use in excess of reimbursement for legitimate and verifiable campaign expenditures and shall expend no funds from his campaign account not attributable to bona fide campaign or political purposes.

7. A Member of the House of Representatives shall treat as campaign contributions all proceeds from testimonial dinners or other fund raising events.

8. A Member or officer of the House of Representatives shall retain no one under his payroll authority who does not perform official duties commensurate with the compensation received in the offices of the employing authority. In the case of committee employees who work under the direct supervision of a Member other than a chairman, the chairman may require that such Member affirm in writing that the employees have complied with the preceding sentence (subject to clause 6 of rule XI) as evidence of the chairman's compliance with this clause and with clause 6 of rule XI.

9. A Member, officer, or employee of the House of Representatives shall not discharge or refuse to hire any individual, or otherwise discriminate against any individual with respect to compensation, terms, conditions, or privileges or employment, because of such individual's race, color, religion, sex (including mari-

tal or parental status), age, or national origin, but may take into consideration the domicile or political affiliation of such individual.

10. A Member of the House of Representatives who has been convicted by a court of record for the commission of a crime for which a sentence of two or more years imprisonment may be imposed should refrain from participation in the business of each committee of which he is a member and should refrain from voting on any question at a meeting of the House, or of the Committee of the Whole House, unless or until judicial or executive proceedings result in reinstatement of the presumption of his innocence or until he is reelected to the House after the date of such conviction.

11. A Member of the House of Representatives shall not authorize or otherwise allow a non-House individual, group, or organization to use the words "Congress of the United States", "House of Representatives", or "Official Business", or any combination of words thereof, on any letterhead or envelope.

12. (a) Except as provided by paragraph (b), any employee of the House of Representatives who is required to file a report pursuant to rule XLIV shall refrain from participating personally and substantially as an employee of the House of Representatives in any contact with any agency of the executive or judicial branch of Government with respect to nonlegislative matters affecting any nongovernmental person in which the employee has a significant financial interest.

(b) Paragraph (a) shall not apply if an employee first advises his employing authority of his significant financial interest and obtains from his employing authority a written waiver stating that the participation of the employee is necessary. A copy of each such waiver shall be filed with the Committee on Standards of Official Conduct.

In addition to this code there are several laws and other rules that limit members' behavior. For a complete list see the Ethics Manual for Members, Officers, and Employees of the U.S. House of Representatives (http://www.house.gov/ethics).

Over the years the House not only developed standards for members' conduct, it also crafted a set of punishments. Expulsion is the most severe punishment and requires a two-thirds vote. The administration of this most severe punishment is quite rare, and only five members have been expelled. Instead, the House has relied more heavily upon censureship as a punishment, having censured twenty-one members since 1832, when the first member was censured. Censuring a member takes a simple majority vote and is the toughest punishment short of expulsion. With censure, members must face their colleagues by standing in the well as the charges against them are read. Starting in 1980, the parties developed rules that removed members who had been censured from leadership posts. In addition to censure, the House may also reprimand its members. Reprimands are generally used for less severe offenses, and members need not be present for a formal dressing down. Reprimands are a more recent form of punishment and have been used eight times since the first reprimand in the House occurred in 1976.[8]

THE ETHICS REFORMS AND
LEGISLATIVE PRINCIPLES

Collectively, these reforms can be seen as a product of the increased attention paid to ethical behavior. Each of the reform efforts followed scandals and arguably reflected the public's desire to clean up government. The results of the focus on ethical legislative behavior have been guidelines for members' actions and a means to enforce those guidelines. However, if these guidelines are to improve the House's ability to function, they should address specific behaviors that harm the House's ability to carry out its duties. Determining whether this is indeed the case can be done by looking at the influence these guidelines have had on the institution's legislative principles (accountability, independence, and fairness) and their ability to prevent the diversion of legislative resources from legislating.

The ethics guidelines that have been promulgated focus largely on behaviors believed to damage the accountability aspect of the legislative process. Indeed, the Obey Commission so recognized the importance of public opinion on this topic that they contracted Lou Harris to conduct a poll (*Cong. Rec.*, 1977, pp. 5894–5896). The poll was used as a means by which the House might know which reforms the American people wanted; it was also used as a justification for specific reforms. For example, the House adopted guidelines that limit transactions between members and interest groups (e.g., limits on honoraria or gifts) to address behaviors the public believed diminish legislators' ability to be accountable. Since Americans also frequently view members of Congress as self-serving and out of touch with real life, the House adopted rules that limit a member's ability to garner perks from office. Financial disclosure and campaign finance reporting requirements have also been adopted with an eye toward increasing accountability by allowing voters to see potential conflicts of interest or threats to members' independence.

Many of the reforms also address the notion of legislative independence. Virtually all reforms that restrict the members' ability to earn money or obtain favors were designed to protect legislative independence. Limits on gifts, honoraria, and travel curtail the potential for members to make policy or other decisions based on who provides them resources instead of the merits of the policies. The prohibition on fiduciary relationships, such as those between lawyer and client in which there is an obligation to work on someone's behalf, helps insure that members' legislative behavior is not affected by such relationships. Even if members do not overtly accept money or gifts in exchange for legislative activities, accepting such gifts could have unintentional consequences and undermine the notion of legislative independence.

Other rules have a clearer connection to behaviors related to the principle of fairness. Limits on the franking privilege prior to elections, for example, are likely to improve fairness. These limits are designed to prevent members from directly using their position for campaign purposes, which most observers acknowledge gives incumbents an unfair advantage. Similarly, standards that prevent members' staffs from doing nonofficial work, including campaigning, help to insure the perception of fairness. Similarly, two of the standards adopted by the House were specifically designed to increase institutional resources by focusing members' devotion to their House work: limits on honoraria and outside earnings. During debates on the 1977 code of conduct, Rep. David Obey (D, WI) noted that the American people wanted full-time members of Congress and that limiting honoraria and outside earnings would limit members' outside activities (*Cong. Rec.*, 1977, pp. 5894–5896). In addition, rules that limit members' use of their staff or other resources for campaign or personal use help to insure that more resources are available for legislating.

While each of the adopted standards address harmful or potentially harmful behaviors, they are far from perfect. From a legislator's standpoint it is often easier to develop rules that prohibit behaviors that are easily identified as ethical errors than it is to develop rules that satisfy some abstract notion of the "ethical legislature." As a result, members who have inappropriate sexual relations or who accept gifts from lobbyists are disciplined regardless of whether their actions influenced their legislative behavior. In fact, Thompson (1995) argues that many of the behaviors that have been addressed under the rubric of ethics reform are not actually harmful to the legislative process. Some types of corruption, particularly individual corruption where the gain is personal and not political, may pose little threat to the legislative process.[9] The ethics reforms of the past have addressed these behaviors because they are relatively easy to detect, not because they clearly violate the principles. Also, some rules contain loopholes. Although members cannot keep personal gifts or accept personal travel, members can skirt gift and travel bans by receiving campaign donations instead of personal gifts (Wayne, 1997).

The desire to curb unethical behavior also may have the unintended effect of hurting the very legislative principles standards are designed to protect. The intent of these reforms was to curb behaviors that damaged public confidence in Congress by improving its accountability to constituents. Whether these reforms had the desired effect of improving public opinion toward Congress is debatable and will be examined in Chapter 3, but many argue that by making unethical behavior punishable, the reforms made them more visible, actually harming American's perceptions of Congress. In addition, the public may actually be less informed about Congressional activities if limits on the frank interfere with the members' ability to communicate with their constituents. Representative Stewart McKinney (R, CT) complained about the franking limits during debates in 1977: "If I wish to communicate with my constituents more than six times in 1 year—and I do—I would be considered prima facie unethical. ... By assuming the worst and legislating against it, do we prevent the best in representation?" (*Cong. Rec.*, 1977, p. 5932).

Finally, it should be noted that the ethics reforms do not address all behaviors that cause harm to the legislative process. The current campaign system is decidedly unfair in that it gives incumbents a clear advantage. Incumbents can roll over money from one election to the next and are better positioned to collect PAC contributions than are challengers. They build large "war chests," which can discourage even the most qualified challengers from running for office. In addition, campaign finance laws still allow members to receive large "gifts" in the form of campaign donations from individuals and businesses who are affected by Congressional action. Although the literature does not tend to find members' behavior greatly influenced by these donations (Grenzke, 1989; Hall & Wayman, 1990; Wawro, 2001; Wright, 1985), such donations appear to have at least the potential to influence members' judgments and harm the accountability of Congress. In addition, other conflicts of interest remain. While a member who owns a business may not vote on legislation directly affecting that business, members who invest in the stock market can still work on legislation to affect the market, doctors vote on legislation dealing with health care, and so on. In addition, while members may sell an interest in an industry they are likely to affect as legislators, that may not fully break the bond they have with that industry.

However, one should not understate the value of the reforms either. Although addressing behaviors that are easily observed instead of those that actually cause harm, and perhaps stopping short of insuring that the legislative obligations will be met, the reforms have value in that they prevent many behaviors that may have resulted in harm to the principles in the first place. Potential conflicts of interest and biases in the system are limited by limiting the size of donations donors can give candidates, by enacting campaign and financial disclosure laws, or by limiting outside earnings. Other reforms, such as limits on outside earnings, limits on the frank, and using staff for nonofficial business, improve fairness. The reforms are not perfect, but that should not be interpreted to mean that the reforms are without merit. The reforms may also have improved behaviors by increasing the odds that members who violate the ethics standards are disciplined.

CHANGES IN BEHAVIOR

Although the reforms are imperfect, they have made tougher ethics rules for members to follow, but that does not necessarily mean that members changed their behaviors. Members may not have ever engaged in the activities that were limited or they may choose to ignore the rules. Nevertheless, Congressional scholars, by and large, believe that members' behavior is more ethical today than in the past. For example, Thompson (1995) states, "However corrupt Congress may be today, few of its members engage in the flagrant behavior that used to be common in the institution. Conduct generally accepted in earlier eras would now be grounds for expulsion. In the nineteenth century respected members openly accepted money for personal use from companies directly affected by the legislation the members supported" (pp. 1–2).

There are several ways the new ethics standards could improve members' behavior. First, the House rules may encourage ethical behavior by simply providing a guide so that members know what is expected of them. A former member of Congress surveyed for this book said, "During my years of service in the Congress, many laws or reform bills were passed to establish the proper code of conduct which members of Congress should adopt or comply with. These have been appropriate standards to establish and I think have served a good purpose. Each member—and our staff—know what is proper—or not proper, or not allowed." Not only do rules serve as a guide to behavior, but the enforcement of the reforms may serve as a deterrent. Members who see other members being disciplined by the chamber or being harassed by the media may wish to avoid the same fate and try to follow the rules. For example, following the investigations of Sen. Thomas Dodd (D, CT) and Rep. Adam Clayton Powell (D, NY) in the 1960s, a member noted that "'everybody reexamined themselves and their procedures'" (Beard and Horn, 1975, p. 70). Members reviewed their procedures and practices to make sure that they would not suffer the same fate that these other members faced. Another way the ethics climate and subsequent reforms may limit unethical behaviors is by removing members who violate the ethics standards. Assuming future behavior is best predicted by past behavior, if the reforms increase the chances that members who violate the standards leave, they are likely to have decreased unethical behavior. Members who are accused of unethical behavior are more likely to lose reelection or retire than are other members.

Having been accused may also affect members' ethical behavior, but it is hard to determine what effect being accused has on members' ethical behavior. On one hand, Sen. John McCain, who was one of the Keating Five, has suggested that because of the scandal he now has to be extra cautious on ethical matters (Doherty, 1998, p. 1359). On the other hand, some members are known repeat offenders. For example, Rep. Charlie H. Wilson (D, CA) was reprimanded in 1978 as part of Koreagate and was censured in 1980 for financial misconduct. The recidivism rate for members who have been accused of unethical behavior may provide an indication of whether members are reformed by the experience of being accused of wrongdoing. About 90 percent of the members who were accused of unethical behavior only faced one accusation.[10] However, since several members left Congress within a couple years of the accusation of corruption or had retired before an accusation took place, they could not be repeat offenders. After removing members who left during the Congress of the accusation, just under 20 percent of the members accused of unethical behavior faced further accusations of unethical behavior. This means that a member who has already been accused of unethical behavior is about twice as likely as be accused again as all members are to ever be accused.

A tempting way to gauge the effects of the ethics climate and reforms on members' behavior is to examine the number of members who violate the ethics rules. Examining the number of House disciplinary actions since 1977 suggests that the ethics climate encouraged unethical, not ethical behavior.[11] Between 1977 and 2002 four members have been censured, seven have been reprimanded, and two have been expelled, for a total of thirteen disciplinary actions in 25 years. This is a higher rate than for the previous 185 years, which saw a total of only twenty-one disciplinary actions.

Making this simple comparison is of limited value. First, prior to 1977 there were fewer rules to violate and no infrastructure to enforce ethical behavior. Thus, members were not disciplined for violating rules because there were few rules. Second, these figures only include violations punished by the House. One problem this creates is that it excludes violations that were pursued only in the courts. The House often chooses to wait to deal with cases that involve legal violations until the judicial system has completed the case, and by the time the judicial process finished the individual may no longer be a member. For example, Rep. Rostenkowski's case was never disciplined by the House because he left Congress before it acted. Another problem is that the House and the House Committee on the Standards of Official Conduct are notorious for having a difficult time convicting members and inflicting punishments. In testimony before the House Ethics Reform Task Force in 1997, Gary Ruskin, director of the Congressional Accountability Project, said, "Unfortunately, the Ethics Committee has become a device to shield members from meaningful scrutiny. It has become an institutional impediment to fair, thorough, credible allegations of wrongdoing. The ethics committee has repeatedly shown a liberal permissiveness towards offenders against House Rules" (U.S. House, 1997, p. 8). Many of the reasons it is difficult for the House to punish its own are related to why the House was reluctant to have rules: *esprit de corps*, partisanship, and believing the voters should determine what is not acceptable. A factor that further complicates discipline decisions is that there can be a fine line between what is acceptable and what is not acceptable (Thompson, 1995, p. 133). This is exemplified in the Keating Five case that occurred in the Senate. In that case, five senators were accused of accepting campaign contributions to put undue pressure on the bureaucracy to help a savings and loan. While the degree of pressure exerted by some of these senators and the possible direct connection between campaign funds was extreme, virtually all members receive money from constituents during campaigns and do favors for them. A final reason members can avoid official discipline is because informal sanctions can be substituted. For example, in 1963, following corruption accusations against Rep. Adam Clayton Powell, the House voted to cut a request Powell made for the Committee on Education and Labor, which he chaired, to study juvenile delinquency. Not only did Congress cut funds, but it took most of the money out of Powell's control and placed it in control of the subcommittees. Therefore, Powell was punished without the House directly acting on his case (Getz, 1966, pp. 104–107). Similarly, Beard and Horn's (1975, p. 67) interviews with fifty members of the House in the 90th Congress led them to conclude that while formal penalties were weak, corrupt members may be ostracized in social settings.

Since counting disciplinary actions in the House serves as a poor indicator of changes in members' behavior, another indicator of changes in members' behavior is used: the number of members accused of violating either House rules or the law. This indicator is an improvement, since it includes legal action as well as Congressional action. This corrects for situations in which a member resigns after an indictment but before the House can take any action. It also is an improvement because it does not require disciplinary action by the House, only an accusation, and includes cases in which a member may have violated the rules but the House did not discipline the member. Of course, this measure has other problems; most notably, it includes cases of members who were exonerated of the accusations.

To estimate changes in the number of accusations of unethical behavior, the number of accusations from 1960 to 1976 is compared with those from 1977 to 2000. This time period was selected since it compares the time following Congress's first effort to set a professional code of conduct for government employees (1958) with that of the time following the more significant changes of the 1970s. To determine changes in the number of accusations over time, I rely on reports of such behavior in *Congressional Quarterly Almanac* from 1960 to 2000. The cases include those that were brought before the Committee on the Standards of Official Conduct (or its precursors) as well as those dealt with in the courts. These sources were used since they not only include official complaints investigated by the ethics committee but also those that were dealt with solely by the courts. It also provides a constant source for the time period examined.

These data indicate a decline in the frequency of unethical behavior. In the sixteen years between 1960 and 1976, 185 individuals were accused of unethical behavior. The number of accusations drops to 119 for the twenty-three-year period between 1977 and 2000.[12] Although the number of known accusations of unethical behavior supports the general wisdom that members are more ethical today, there are problems with these data. Most notably, if there is variation in the willingness of people to make accusations, then the data are not comparable. Although both time periods include the ethics climate, the willingness of members to make allegations against each other has waxed and waned. For example, since the 105th Congress members' willingness to make charges of unethical behavior against each other has declined. In the 107th Congress, Democrats were able to prevent Republicans from bringing charges against one of their own by threatening Majority Whip Tom Delay with charges of unethical behavior (Bresnahan, 2002). Second, throughout the period the behaviors that were considered inappropriate changed. For example, today a member who pockets honoraria would be violating House rules and would likely face an accusation of unethical behavior. However, twenty years ago it was not a violation of any rule and considered acceptable behavior. Thus, another indicator of changes in members' behavior is used: members' perceptions of the frequency of behaviors.

Members' Perceptions

One way to try to gauge changes in members' behavior may be simply to ask them to compare the frequency of certain behaviors before and after the ethics reforms. The value of asking individual members is that they are aware of their own behavior and may be aware of others' behavior as well. However, a likely problem with this approach is that members may give socially desirable responses. They may not want themselves or their colleagues to appear corrupt or as underreporting violations. They might also have forgotten or altered their perceptions with the passage of time. Nevertheless, this may be the best available indicator of changes in rank and file members' behavior.

To estimate members' perceptions of changes in the frequency of behaviors addressed by the reforms, a survey of former members of the House who entered the House in or prior to 1977 and left in or after 1985 was conducted. To get addresses for these members, the 1997–98 Directory of the United States Association of Former Members of Congress was used. The surveys were sent in the summer of 1998 and contained both open-ended and closed questions concerning members' impressions of changes in the frequency of specific behaviors and the costs and values of the reforms (see Appendix B for a copy of the instrument). Only 39 of the 107 members sent surveys responded. One reason for the relatively poor response rate was that some former members were in ill health and simply not able to respond (remember, the members surveyed had served in the House prior to 1977). Given the low response rate, the findings may not reflect the views of all members, and the findings should be seen as suggestive. On the plus side, however, the sample did include a good mix of members. They varied in terms of party identification, number of years served, and region of residence. Respondents also differed in their experiences with ethics violations. While most respondents had not been accused of violating House ethics, some of the respondents had been accused of ethical missteps.

Members were asked three types of questions to help estimate changes in members' behavior. First, members were asked to specify if and how they changed their behaviors to comply with the reforms. If members noted that their behaviors changed, it provided confirmation of improved ethics. Similarly, members were asked to specify if they knew others who altered their behaviors and which behaviors were altered. These questions were designed to help minimize the likelihood that members would offer socially desirable responses. One way to limit socially desirable responses is to soften the context (Dillman, 1978, p. 106). To soften the context, members were asked about the behavior of members other than the respondent. This enabled respondents to avoid having to admit that they violated today's ethics standard earlier in their careers. Third, members were asked their impressions about how common certain behaviors were at different time periods. Members were given a list of eleven behaviors that were at least partially addressed in the code of conduct. They were then asked how common these behaviors were during five different time periods: 1965 to 1970, 1971 to 1976, 1977 to 1983, 1984 to 1990, and 1991 to 1996. These data indicate whether there were alterations to specific behaviors and when those changes took place. By knowing when changes took place it is possible to estimate whether they correspond to the reforms. Members were asked to note if they did not serve in a given time period.[13]

The findings support the view that members' behavior today is more ethical than in the past. A majority of respondents (55%) specifically stated that they personally altered their behaviors in order to comply with the rules. In addition, many others noted some minor change that they made or said they never had done anything dishonest. The most common changes that members admitted to making were no longer accepting honoraria and limiting their outside incomes. A couple of others noted that they resigned from corporation boards or sold stock.

A majority of respondents (53%) were also aware of others who changed their behavior to comply with the ethics reforms. Generally, they reported that other members stopped accepting honoraria, or that members changed to comply with the new rules in an unspecified way. That a large minority of respondents did not indicate that other members changed their behavior is not necessarily an indication that change did not occur. Several of these members noted that they simply lacked knowledge about others' behavior.

The third set of questions also provides evidence of changing behaviors. Table 2.4 presents information on changes in specific behaviors. Since the indicators are ordinal, each cell presents the mean and median score for respondents' perceptions of how common certain behaviors were during a time period, with a 10 indicating the behavior was very common and a 1 indicating it was not common. In the table the eleven behaviors were divided into three groups according to their potential to harm the legislative process. The first group, which includes sexual misconduct and converting campaign monies to personal monies, create a category likely to have the least potential to cause harm to the legislative process.[14] They were likely to harm accountability if detected but were not likely to harm the independence or fairness principles, nor were they likely to decrease legislative resources. The second category is comprised of activities that not only harm the accountability principle, but have the potential to harm members' ability to meet the other two principles, fairness and independence. The activities included in this category were having a financial interest in business affected by Congressional action, behaving in a manner that reflects poorly on the House, earning large outside incomes, and receiving trips, honoraria, and gifts. The third category included activities directly linked to fairness, independence, or decreasing legislative resources.

Table 2.4
Prevalence of Behaviors over Time

	1965–1970			1971–1976			1977–1983			1984–1990			1991–1996		
	Ȳ	M*	N**	Ȳ	M*	N**	Ȳ	M*	N**	Ȳ	M*	N**	Ȳ	M*	N**
Minor effects on the legislative process															
Converted campaign dollars to personal use	3.3	[2]	(8)	3.9	[2]	(21)	3.7	[4]	(24)	3.8	[3]	(21)	2.4	[2]	(11)
Sexual misconduct	1.9	[1.5]	(7)	2.3	[1]	(18)	1.9	[1]	(22)	1.8	[1]	(20)	1.4	[1]	(11)
Potentially significant effects															
Behaved in a manner that did not reflect credibly on the House	1.5	[1]	(7)	2.0	[1]	(19)	1.9	[1.5]	(23)	2.0	[2]	(20)	2.4	[1.5]	(10)
Had large outside earnings	3.6	[3.5]	(7)	3.8	[4]	(19)	3.8	[3]	(22)	3.3	[2.5]	(19)	2.8	[1]	(9)
Had a financial interest in legislation	2.5	[2]	(7)	2.9	[2.5]	(18)	2.7	[2]	(21)	2.8	[2]	(18)	3.1	[1.5]	(10)
Received gifts from interest groups	2.3	[2]	(6)	3.3	[2]	(17)	2.2	[1]	(21)	2.1	[1]	(18)	1.1	[1]	(8)
Received honoraria	4.5	[3]	(8)	6.4	[5]	(20)	7.0	[8]	(23)	7.2	[8.5]	(20)	2.3	[1]	(8)
Travel reimbursed by interest groups	4.3	[3]	(7)	6.2	[6.5]	(20)	6.0	[7]	(24)	6.4	[7]	(21)	5.5	[5]	(11)
Likely significant effects															
Appeared intoxicated on the floor	1.4	[2]	(6)	1.8	[1]	(18)	1.5	[1]	(22)	1.5	[1]	(19)	1.0	[1]	(9)
Misused the frank	2.4	[1.5]	(7)	3.4	[1]	(19)	3.5	[2]	(23)	3.5	[3]	(19)	3.0	[1.5]	(10)
Misused staff	3.9	[5]	(8)	3.8	[2]	(20)	3.2	[3]	(24)	3.0	[3]	(21)	3.0	[3]	(11)

Note: The range for responses was from 1 to 10, with 10 indicating that the activity was very common and 1 indicating that it was not common.

*Medians.

**Number of cases. They vary due to missing data.

This category included being intoxicated on the floor and using staff or the frank for campaigning. Using legislative resources for campaigning gave these incumbents an unfair advantage during elections, and being intoxicated on the floor and using staff for personal gain or campaigning involved using legislative resources for nonlegislative functions and may affect fairness. Member's and staff's time are considered resources.

Examining the activities in these categories indicate that each category saw a decline in members' unethical behaviors. The behaviors that more clearly affected the legislative principles show a decline just as those that only affected accountability. However, the category where members' perceived the greatest decline is the middle category: the potential to cause harm. This is consistent with the argument made by many that the reforms addressed behaviors that have the potential to cause harm more so than limiting actual harm.

Respondents reported reductions in two behaviors thought to have the least effect on the legislative process: converting campaign dollars to personal use and sexual misconduct. Respondents believed that it was fairly common for members to convert campaign dollars to personal use prior to the 1990s. However, following the early 1990 reforms that prohibited converting campaign funds to personal funds, members perceived such conversion to be less common. Members also reported lower levels of sexual misconduct in the 1990s than in earlier times, although sexual misconduct was never perceived as a common behavior on Capitol Hill.

The survey data indicate that there was a noticeable decline in the behaviors thought to have a potential to harm the legislative process. First, members noted that the frequency of members receiving large gifts from interest groups declined after the reforms of the early 1990s. Although during the early 1970s the average respondent gave receiving gifts a 3 on the 10-point scale, the average fell to 1.1 by the 1990s. The change in the frequency of honoraria was larger. Prior to the change in the rules that made pocketing honoraria a violation of House rules, members thought it was common for members to receive honoraria (around 7 on the 10-point scale). During the 1990s, however, they perceived the activity as quite uncommon (2.3). Respondents also saw a decline in members' travel sponsored by interest groups. After the reforms, members cut down on accepting travel from interest groups. Although lower than in early time periods, since the rule allows for some travel, the frequency of members receiving trips remained fairly high. Respondents also saw a modest decline in the frequency with which members received large outside incomes. Prior to the 1980s, members reported moderate levels of large outside earnings. During the 1980s and 1990s, they reported a modest decline in members' receiving large outside earnings.

Two behaviors with the potential to harm the legislative process, however, did not see a decline in their frequency.[15] Respondents believed that it is more common today than in the past for members to have a financial stake in Congressional actions. They also believed it was more common in the 1990s for members not to behave credibly on the floor. The increase in these behaviors likely reflects changes in the makeup of Congress. During the 1990s, as more members from a business background entered the House, it is likely that they would have economic interests affected by policies, or their family and friends could have such interests. Similarly, as fewer career politicians are elected they have less interest in following norms such as courtesy or seeing value in improving the image of Congress. In fact, many gained their positions by feeding on the generally high disapproval ratings of Congress.

The behaviors most likely to harm the legislative process have generally seen modest declines since the 1960s. Members generally reported low levels of intoxication on the floor for all periods of time, but it was least common in the 1990s. Respondents perceived similar declines in misusing the staff. Changes in misusing the frank declined in the 1990s but is at a higher level today than forty years ago, as there was a large increase in misusing the frank in the late 1960s.

The observed decline in members' unethical behaviors coincided with changes in House rules to address those abuses. Between 1965 and 1971, when there were no significant rule changes, there was not a consistent decline in the behaviors. In fact, there was a rise in the frequency of several behaviors that today violate ethics rules. Members were more likely to accept gifts, honoraria, and travel from interest groups immediately after 1971 than they were prior to it.[16] They also were more likely to misuse the frank and not behave in a manner that reflected well on the House. However, following 1977, the year the code of conduct was enacted, these behaviors started to diminish. Only receiving honoraria became more common after 1977 than prior to it, and the 1977 reforms did not address honoraria. Then, following the 1989 reforms, respondents again reported a decline in several of the unethical behaviors, particularly those behaviors that were part of the 1989 rules. Most notably, members became significantly less likely to accept gifts, honoraria, and trips, and to convert campaign dollars into personal use (following 1992 members could no longer pocket their campaign dollars when they retired).

Although Table 2.4 generally supports the idea that these behaviors declined over the years, the decline was not dramatic. Most of the unethical behaviors were never common. As one member surveyed for this project put it, "While Congress like every pursuit has an occasional 'Bad Apple' . . . my greatest surprise was finding the very high level of integrity, ability and dedication of the average congressman on both sides of the aisle." Another member, who served for twenty years, said that the system works well and is the least corrupt in the world. Others echoed these sentiments, saying most members are dedicated to serving the people and are not corrupt.

The only behaviors that members saw as common (more than a 5 on the 10-point scale) were receiving honoraria and travel from interest groups. Both of these have legitimate official value, by encouraging members to gain and give information. Thus, while they have the potential to bias members' judgment, they also have the potential for increased representation and improved policy making. In fact, not all travel, honoraria, or use of the frank have been banned, in part, for this reason.

CONCLUSION

Over the past fifty years, the House has gone from not having a code of conduct to developing a code, additional laws and rules to insure ethical behavior, and an infrastructure to enforce the rules. This has led to the punishment of dozens of members. While the codes contain loopholes, they do address many behaviors that potentially harm the legislative process. The reforms limit members' potential for making decisions based on financial gain instead of the merits of the issue at hand; they also instruct members to refuse money that could bias their decision making and limit some unfairness by regulating the use of the frank and staff for nonofficial purposes. The reforms, however, do not address all potential abuses. Many argue that the current campaign financing system provides an unfair advantage to incumbents over challengers, decreases legislative accountability, and has the potential for biasing members' decisions. Thus, while the reforms were a step toward improving members' behavior, they were incomplete, allowing some abuses to continue.

Although imperfect, the reforms have improved members' behaviors. Members perceive a decline in most of the behaviors that the reforms were designed to address. The timing of the changes in behavior also suggests that the adoption of a code of conduct contributed to the improvements in members' behavior, as members' behaviors changed immediately following the reforms. This chapter also suggests that behaviors that are disruptive to the legislative process and divert resources away from legislating have decreased. Thus, the ethics climate and the House code have improved the ability of the House to function by improving members' behavior. As one of the former members surveyed said, "There is no question but that the ethics reforms of recent years have improved the opportunity for Congress to do a better job in the public's best interests. The abolition of honoraria, limitation on outside income, and restrictions of gifts are all steps in the right direction. There is still much that can be done to make the system better."

This chapter finds evidence that the reforms had the desired effect of improving members' ethics. Although the reforms are not perfect, they provide tougher standards than what preceded them and members by and large comply with those standards. The next chapter explores whether the new standards improved the public's confidence in Congress or had the unintended consequence of focusing the public's attention on the violations of the ethics standards.

NOTES

1. As a senator, Torricelli faced his own ethics battle. He was accused, but never indicted, of accepting campaign money in exchange for favors in his 1996 Senate bid. In 2002 the Senate ethics panel did admonish him.

2. Wilson (1951) noted that before ethics standards could be improved it would be necessary to treat those in politics by standards other than those applied to individuals in society at large.

3. Getz (1966, p. 24) lists investigations into the following: five-percenters, Kefauver Crime Committee, Reconstruction Finance Corporation, Maritime Commission, Bureau of Internal Revenue, and senatorial campaign practice. In addition, in 1957–1958 there was an investigation of federal regulatory agencies.

4. Rep. Robert Sikes (D, FL) was reprimanded for violating disclosure and conflict of interest codes. Rep. Wayne Hays (D, OH) was reported to have put Elizabeth Ray on the government payroll for sexual favors. Rep. Andrew Hinshaw (R, CA) was sent to prison for bribery. Rep. James Jones (D, OK) pleaded guilty to failing to report a contribution. Rep. Henry Helstoski (D, NJ) was indicted for bribery. Rep. Allan Howe (D, UT) was convicted of soliciting sex. Rep. James Hastings (R, NY) was indicted for a kickback scheme. Several House members had trips to hunting lodges as guests of military contractors (*Congressional Ethics*, 1980).

5. In many ways this law was also in response to a scandal. This time the scandal involved the accounting practices of several large corporations that went bankrupt. Many members of Congress had accepted large campaign donations from these corporations.

6. The revolving door refers to the practice of members leaving Congress and taking lucrative jobs as lobbyists or bureaucrats.

7. In 1997, following the reprimand of Speaker Gingrich, the House did pass new procedures for the investigation of ethics, giving the committee a nonpartisan staff and requiring nonmembers to get a member to sponsor a complaint.

8. In addition, the House has rebuked, condemned, fined, taken away leadership positions, and reduced seniority as forms of punishment. These are seen as less severe or less common than reprimands and may not require a vote by the chamber.

9. For an interesting discussion on the difficulty in condemning personal gain from political office, see Andrew Stark (1997).

10. See Chapter 6 to determine who was accused of unethical behavior.

11. The 1977 cutoff is used since this was the year the House enacted the new codes, so it is a milestone in ethics standards. Although the rules have been altered since 1977, 1977 distinguishes a period of virtually no official standards from a period of standards.

12. Using the term "individuals" accused may be somewhat misleading, as some members were accused in different congresses for different offenses. However, the term is used since some cases involved multiple members. For example, in 1970 Ford Motor Company leased Lincolns at considerably reduced rates for nineteen members of Congress. This would only be one case, but it involved nineteen members. Examining the number of cases, instead of individuals, would also suggest a decrease in unethical behavior. In the pre-1977 reform period there were four cases involving multiple members, including a total of eighty-five members, and in the postreform period there

were five multimember cases involving forty-four members (Abscam, Koreagate, House bank, Page-Sex, and drug investigation).

13. The data from period to period at some level are not comparable since some differences exist in the individuals responding from one period to the next. Thus, I also examined individual members' responses to see if they demonstrated the same pattern discussed. Generally they do. Fourteen members' responses indicate they saw declines in the behaviors following the reforms, compared to four members who saw an increase and seven who generally saw no change.

14. The question did not specify whether the sexual misconduct involved staff members; if it did, sexual misconduct would involve depleting legislative resources and could affect the fairness principle.

15. However, there was not an increase in the median score for the degree of members having "financial interest in legislation."

16. The rise, interestingly, corresponds to the rise of interest groups and political action committees.

CHAPTER 3

The Effects of the Ethics Climate on Public Attitudes Toward Congress

One goal of the ethics reforms was to improve the public's image of Congress. As Representative David Obey (D, WI) stated during debate on the 1977 reform bill, drafted by the committee bearing his name, "I think it is important that we understand that what we are trying to do here is to draft a code of ethics today which simply reflects what our public responsibilities are so that we can have public confidence in at least the integrity of the processes around here" (*Cong. Rec.*, 1977, p. 5896). But whether it accomplished this goal is in debate. It is likely that the ethics climate and reforms increased the appearance of a Congress ripe with unethical behaviors, since by creating rules for members to violate it highlighted violations and made them public. This chapter examines the effects of the ethics reforms and the ethics climate on the public's approval of Congress by examining the effects of ethics violations and the conviction of those accused on Congressional approval ratings.

Low public approval can be detrimental to Congress and, more generally, the entire political system. Therefore, whether ethics violations affect the public's approval of Congress is critical to understand. Not only is the public's confidence related to the accountability principle, but David Easton (1986) has argued that voluntary support of government institutions is essential to the survival and strength of democracy. For citizens to willingly follow laws and provide the requisite resources to the government, they must support the political system. When the system loses the support of its citizens, the system is in jeopardy of having to rely on coercion. There are other issues as well. A system lacking sufficient support cannot attract quality candidates to run for office. Parker (1996) has argued that as public approval of Congress declines, members who sought office for prestige reasons are likely to leave. Instead of members seeking public service, an institution lacking public support is more likely to attract legislators seeking to profit (e.g., financial gain or lucrative post-Congressional careers) from elective office. The potential consequence of this pattern does not bode well for the future of the institution. Instead of a legislative body populated by politicians wishing to serve for the public's good, the institution becomes composed of those who are willing to privately profit from service in an unpopular institution (Parker, 1996, p. 90).

A system that lacks support and is perceived as unethical may also have a difficult time mustering support for another necessary systemic input: voting (but see Patterson & Barr, 1995, p. 287). The benefits of voting are likely to be diminished in political systems perceived as unethical. Americans motivated to vote by a strong sense of civic duty are less likely to feel a duty to participate in a tainted system. In fact, there is some evidence that negative campaign advertising, ads that "criticize, discredit, or belittle their opponents," decreases voter turnout (Ansolabehere, Iyengar, Simon, & Valentino, 1994, p. 829; also see Ansolabeher, Iyengar, & Simon, 1999; but see Goldstein & Freedman, 2002). Negative advertising is similar to ethics violations, since both point out the worst in politicians and can make the process and the actors appear unworthy of our trust. Declines in voter turnout harm the democratic nature of the system, since some voices are not heard.

Finally, a political system that is lacking the public's support and seen as unethical may have a difficult time persuading its citizens to voluntarily adhere to the rule of law. There are two ways to gain citizens' compliance with the law: instrumental and normative (Tyler, 1990). Instrumental compliance involves using punishment as a deterrent to violating the law and normative can involve either moral agreement with the law or a belief that the law is legitimate. According to Tyler (1990) the latter is the most efficient way to gain compliance because it does not require police to enforce the law nor people to agree with the law. There is also evidence that people who see the government (or the legal branch) as legitimate are more likely to follow it (Tyler, 1990) and less likely to engage in violent protest (Worchel, Hester, & Kopala, 1974). Events at the end of the twentieth century seem to support this view as well. The growth of the militia movements in the 1990s was the result of those who questioned the legitimacy of the government's actions. Members of militias believe that the government is corrupt and conspires against the average American. Consequently, these citizens believe they have a right, if not a responsibility, to be prepared to defend the ideals of the Constitution, perhaps by literally attacking the government. On a less extreme note, Cohen and Copeland (1997, pp. 19–20) found that people who were aware of and upset by the House banking scandal had high levels of support for term-limits proposals, which supporters contend will clean up and limit government.

Whether ethics violations cause the types of problems mentioned here depends on the degree to which the violations decrease approval and whether the public's views toward the institution or its members are affected. If unethical behaviors damage the public's views toward the general membership but do not alter perceptions of the institution, the negative effects of violations may be minimized. Even if the membership is not fully trustworthy, an institution or process that is ethical may be seen as offering protection against the membership. Although negative views of the membership may discourage Americans from wanting to serve in Congress, it will not likely result in delegitimizing legislative decisions, since the process and procedures are viewed as legitimate.

WHY ETHICS VIOLATIONS AFFECT PUBLIC CONFIDENCE

For the ethics climate and reforms to cause the types of problems mentioned here they would have to affect public opinion. The argument offered here is that the reforms affect public opinion because they make violations known.[1] When rules and an infrastructure to enforce rules are established, behaviors that violate those rules are discovered and prosecuted. Without the rules there are no violations to make public. Prior to the reforms, members' unethical behaviors did not damage the public's opinion about Congress because they were invisible to the public. The literature on American's attitudes toward Congress offers reasons to expect violations to harm the public's approval of Congress. Kimball and Patterson (1997) argue that when citizens' expectations about Congress are not met, approval ratings fall. The public has expectations about how members of Congress ought to behave, and when they fail to live up to those expectations, the public's disappointment translates into disapproval of Congress. Kimball and Patterson also discovered that citizens expect members to adhere to high ethical standards, which means that even minor ethical transgressions can translate into negative evaluations of Congress.

Not only does violating ethics standards in a general sense violate the public's expectations, but since ethics violations may actually make Congress function more poorly, it further harms the public's support for the institution. Unethical behavior harms the legislative process because it prevents legislators from meeting their obligations of independence, fairness, and accountability (see Chapters 1 and 2; Hastings Center, 1985; Thompson, 1995 for a discussion of these principles and how the reforms relate to them). Hibbing and Theiss-Morse's (1995) research can fit within this line of reasoning. They find that Americans' attitudes toward Congress are affected by the process. Americans in the early 1990s had low approval toward Congress because they did not like the conflict and compromise needed in a democratic institution. Certainly, as the ethics investigations have played out they have caused conflict. In essence, a process that allows unethical behavior does not meet Americans' expectations and thus decreases their approval of Congress.

The research on Congressional approval also provides empirical evidence that unethical behavior, scandals, or corruption can have a negative effect on Congressional approval. Patterson and Magleby (1992) noted that the lowest period for Congressional approval corresponded with Koreagate and the House banking scandal. Similarly, Durr, Gilmour, & Wolbrecht (1997) found that the House banking scandal had a strong negative effect on public opinion and Koreagate a modest effect. However, they also found some scandals (Keating Five, Speaker Wright's resignation, Abscam, and the Post Office scandal) had no significant effect on public opinion. Similarly, Hibbing and Theiss-Morse (1995, pp. 69–71) and Patterson and Barr (1995) found that the House banking scandal in 1992 contributed to Americans' negative feelings for Congress. Using a different approach, Patterson and Caldeira (1990) found that the frequency of news reports of ethics violations affected the public's approval of Congress such that as the number of stories increased, public approval fell.

Although these studies found at least some effect of ethics violations on public opinion, they did not focus on the effects that the violations had on Americans' support for Congress, nor did they address key issues involved in the relationship. They did not examine whether disciplining members (as opposed to accusing members) independently affected public support. Disciplining members may have a positive effect. It may indicate that the system does not tolerate unethical behavior, or that the system is fair. If disciplining members has this effect it would indicate the reforms have had a positive effect on accountability because the reforms allow for discipline. The studies also failed to examine whether violations harm support for Congress the institution or support for the membership, or both. This issue is important because it suggests the degree to which the negative effects ethics violations cause to public opinion are a real threat to the system and how Congress may react to ethics violations to minimize their negative effects. This chapter examines these unexplored effects of ethics violations on public opinion.

EFFECTS OF ETHICS VIOLATIONS
ON PUBLIC OPINION

This section examines the effects of ethics violations on public approval of Congress, and whether disciplining members has an independent effect. Each of these questions helps improve our understanding of the effects of the ethics reforms on the accountability function. If violations harm the public's approval of Congress, the reforms and the ethics climate harmed accountability by making violations visible. Also, if the public's approval of Congress is improved when Congress disciplines members who violate the ethics standard, the ethics reforms may have had some positive effects on Congressional approval by increasing the odds that members are disciplined. Congress can regain some of the loss in public approval caused by ethics violations by disciplining a member for wrongdoing.

To estimate the effect that ethics violations have on public approval, Durr et al.'s (1997) measure of public approval ratings was used. These data provide a quarterly estimate of public approval of Congress from 1974 to 1993.[2] It combines the results of numerous surveys and was based on Stimson's "dyad ratios" algorithm (see Durr et al., 1997, pp. 178–182 for a discussion of the data).[3]

Besides estimating the public's approval of Congress, it is necessary to estimate ethics violations. To measure whether ethics violations are likely to affect public opinion at a particular time, I rely on the number of stories reported in the *New York Times* that discussed an accusation of unethical behavior implicating members of either the House or the Senate.[4] Coverage of ethics violations involving both chambers was used, since the polling questions concerning Congressional approval do not distinguish between the chambers. This measure is similar to the one used by Patterson and Caldeira (1990). Using news stories instead of a dichotomous measure of whether an investigation of a violation was present was used for several reasons. First, the more news coverage a violation receives the more likely Americans are to be aware of it, and for violations to affect public approval ratings the public needs to be aware of them. Second, there is likely a relationship between the number of stories and the importance of the story, at least as defined by the editors.[5] These data were coded quarterly from 1974 to 1993 to correspond to the data on public approval.

Disciplining a member for unethical behavior may have an effect on public opinion that is independent from the effects of the violation per se. It is possible that Congress taking a strong disciplinary action against one of its own might have negative effects on Congressional approval. Such formal actions typically garner media coverage that feeds the public's skepticism of Congress. However, it is more likely that disciplining members would have positive effects on approval ratings. First, it makes the system appear fair. A member who violated the standards did not evade punishment. The disciplinary action may also be perceived by the public as a sign that the system does not tolerate unethical behavior and stands ready to discipline a member who violates the ethics standards. Moreover, the action marks an end to the scandal and the publicity surrounding it, allowing Congress to get back to its job of legislating. To estimate the effects of disciplining unethical behavior on public approval, the number of *New York Times* stories covering the disciplining of a member who violated the code of ethics by a vote in the House or to have violated the law by the criminal system in each quarter from 1974 to 1993 was measured.[6] Coverage of the discipline was used, since to affect the public's approval the public has to be aware of the action.

To estimate the effects of disciplining members and news coverage of ethics violations on public opinion I used Ordinary Least Squares (OLS) regression.[7] This allows for the effects of different variables to be controlled when testing this relationship. To insure that the model does a reasonable job explaining variation in public approval ratings, several control variables were used. The controls are the variables that Durr et al. (1997) found significantly related to their approval measure.[8] These variables include major bills passed, internal conflict in Congress, previous quarter's approval ratings, the number of vetoes, the number of overrides, and expectations about the economy.

The means for all the variables are listed in Table 3.1. During the twenty-year period there was an average of 17.78 stories on unethical behavior in each quarter, and approval ratings were 65 percent. There was great variation in these variables. The largest number of stories in one quarter was 61 and the least 0. Approval ratings also varied greatly, ranging from 49 to 80 percent. These figures do not indicate any clear increase in reporting of violations over the twenty years. The *New York Times* gave great coverage to violations involving leaders or multiple members and less coverage to individual violations. On average every third quarter a story reported on the disciplining of a member. The most disciplinary actions taken in one quarter were five in the fourth quarter of 1980 and corresponded with Abscam. The economic expectations averaged .81. Just under one and a half ma-

Table 3.1
Means and Standard Deviations for News Coverage, Congressional Approval, and Variables Thought to Affect Approval, 1974 to 1993

	Mean	S.D.
Violations coverage	17.78	15.88
Disciplinary action	.34	.76
Approval (t1)	64.53	8.20
Approval (t-1)	64.68	8.14
Economic expectation	80.62	12.61
Major bills	1.41	1.54
Vetoes	4.44	5.68
Overrides	.29	.80
Internal conflict	4.01	3.15

Source: Much of the data used here were taken from "Explaining Congressional Approval," by R. H. Durr, J. B. Gilmour, and C. Wolbrecht, 1997, *American Journal of Political Science*, *41*, pp. 75–207.

Key: Violation coverage: number of stories in the *New York Times* about members' ethics violations.

Disciplinary action: number of stories in the *New York Times* reporting that a member had been disciplined.

Approval (t1): average approval ratings of Congress in a quarter.

Approval (t-1): approval rate in the previous quarter.

Economic expectations: a measure of consumer sentiment ranging from 0 to 100.

Major bills: number of major bills in a quarter.

Vetoes: number of presidential vetoes in a quarter.

Overrides: number of times Congress overrode a presidential veto in a quarter.

Internal conflict: number of cloture votes and debt ceiling bills.

jor bills were passed a quarter. There were on average 4 vetoes and .29 overrides, and the institutional conflict average was 4.

Table 3.2 presents the results from a regression equation estimating the effects of ethics violations on approval ratings. Overall the model explains 86 percent of the variance in approval ratings. The model also finds that unethical behaviors affect approval ratings as expected. When the *New York Times* reported on unethical behaviors, the public's approval of Congress fell (b = – .06, p = .02). Thus, for every story on unethical behavior printed in the *New York Times* in a quarter, approval ratings fell .06 percent. Although this means that a few stories will not have a noticeable effect on approval ratings, in the quarter when there were sixty-one stories the approval ratings were estimated to fall 3.7 points. For ethics violations that were reported over several quarters, their effects may be significant. For example, since the *New York Times* printed seventy-nine stories on the House banking scandal, the findings indicate the scandal caused about a 5-percent drop in approval ratings.

Table 3.2 also indicates that when a member was disciplined, approval ratings rose. The relationship was statistically significant but the substantive effect was fairly modest. Every time a story reported that a member was disciplined, Congress regained 1 percent in its approval rating. This indicates that by increasing the chances that members are disciplined the reform may have had some positive effects on public opinion. It also indicates that as an institution Congress

Table 3.2
Effects of News Coverage of Ethics Violations on Congressional Approval, 1974 to 1993

	B	S.E.
Violations coverage	−.06	.02**
Disciplinary action	1.02	.53*
Approval (t-1)	.87	.05***
Economic expectation	.03	.03
Major bills	−.37	.31
Vetoes	.15	.10+
Overrides	−.97	.60+
Internal conflict	−.22	.12*
Constant	7.85	3.90**

Source: Much of the data used here were taken from "Explaining Congressional Approval," by R. H. Durr, J. B. Gilmour, and C. Wolbrecht, 1997, *American Journal of Political Science, 41*, pp. 75–207.

R^2 = .86; Adj. R^2 = .84; n = 79

+ < .20; * < .10; ** < .05; *** < .01 (two-tailed test)

can behave in a way to recoup some of the public's confidence that was lost after a scandal became public: swiftly discipline the member for wrongdoing.

These data indicate that ethics violations have a noticeable but not dramatic effect on public approval ratings. While there is a statistically significant effect of news stories on approval ratings, it would take almost seventeen news stories in the *New York Times* to lower approval ratings 1 percent. This decline of approval would be erased if the House took action against a member who violated the ethical standards.

THE NATURE OF THE DECLINE IN CONGRESSIONAL APPROVAL

These findings, while instructive in revealing the effects of ethics violations and disciplining members on approval ratings, only tell part of the story. The part of the story that is left out is where citizens place the blame for unethical behaviors: with the members or with the institution. Determining the target of the public's disapproval is important, since it would shed light on the degree to which ethics violations harm the legitimacy of the institution. If the greatest effect of ethics violations is on the evaluations of the institution, the system's legitimacy is in greater jeopardy than if the evaluations of the membership are affected. Negative evaluations of the membership are harmful if they decrease the willingness of members to serve; however, this harm is less than if the whole institution is seen as unethical. In this case, citizens may feel little value in supporting the institution and the laws that come out of it. If the membership is perceived as unethical by the public but the institution is perceived as ethical, citizens are still likely to support the laws and system generally. To estimate whether the public's approval of the membership, the institution, or both suffer from ethics violations, a cross-sectional survey conducted by John R. Hibbing and Elizabeth Theiss-Morse (1995) was used.[10] The national survey was conducted between July and October 1992. The survey queried 1,433 Americans and was designed to measure attitudes, beliefs, and feelings about Congress. It is ideal for this project, since it was designed to determine if the public held separate attitudes for the members and for the institutional structure of the Congress.

To measure how ethics violations affect the public's perceptions of members of Congress and of the institution itself, four questions were utilized. First, respondents were asked their feelings toward members and the institution using two feeling thermometer questions. These questions asked respondents to place their feelings toward Congress as the institution from 100 (warm feelings) to 0 (cold feelings), and then asked to place their feelings toward Congressional membership using the same scale. As Hibbing and Theiss-Morse (1995) reported, the public holds warmer feelings for the institution than it does for the members of Congress (see Table 3.3). Similarly, the public's approval of the membership was estimated by asking respondents, "Again, thinking about people in government, please tell me if you strongly approve, approve,

Table 3.3
Means and Standard Deviations for Data on Americans' Feelings and Evaluations of Congress

	Means	S.D.
Feeling thermometer		
Member	41.78	18.64
Institution	65.69	23.85
Approval		
Member	2.06	.65
Institution	3.06	.58
Concern for ethics	.99	.29
Interest	3.20	.81
Sex	.53	.50
Party	.33	.47
Efficacy	1.38	1.07
Knowledge	6.15	1.45
Education	5.22	2.04

Source: The data used here were collected in *Congress as Public Enemy: Public Attitudes toward American Political Institutions*, by J. R. Hibbing, and E. Theiss-Morse, 1995, New York: Cambridge University Press.

Concern for ethics: combination score; see text (0 = not concerned with ethics, 2 = concerned with ethics)

Key: Interest: 1 = not at all interested; 4 = very interested

Sex: 0 = male; 1 = female

Party: 1 = Democrat; 0 = other

Efficacy: 0 = low efficacy; 3 = high efficacy

Knowledge: 0 = low knowledge; 8 = high knowledge

Education: 1 = less than high school; 8 = graduate degree

Feeling member: feeling thermometer about members

Feeling institution: feeling thermometer about institution

Approval member: 1 = strongly disapprove; 4 = strongly approve

Approval institution: 1 = strongly disapprove; 4 = strongly approve

disapprove, or strongly disapprove of the way the people are handling their jobs. What about the 535 members of Congress?" Finally, measuring approval of the institution was ascertained with the following question: "I have a few more questions about the institutions of the government in Washington—that is, the Presidency, the Supreme Court, and Congress. In general, do you strongly approve, approve, disapprove, or strongly disapprove. . . . What about the U.S. Congress, no matter who is in office?"

Both feeling thermometer questions and both approval questions were examined, since they measure different types of reactions. The questions measuring approval are most similar to those examined in the previous section of this chapter and most likely reflect respondents' cognitive evaluations of either the 535 members or the institutional structures. The feeling thermometer questions, however, allow respondents to position themselves on a larger scale and tap their affective feelings toward members of Congress and the institution. Understanding citizens' feelings about Congress as well as their cognitive evaluations is important, since both are likely to influence their support for the membership or institution. The question here is not, however, whether ethics violations influence feelings more than cognitions, but whether ethics violations affect the public's reactions (feelings or evaluations) more toward Congress's membership or the institution.

The primary aim here is to examine the influence that ethics violations have on the public's support for Congress. Unfortunately, the Hibbing and Theiss-Morse (1995) survey does not directly ask respondents to comment on ethics violations or how such violations alter their perceptions of members and the institution. Instead, two items are combined to create a measure of the respondents' concern with members' ethics. The first question asked respondents to react to a specific problem (the House banking scandal) and how that event might have shaped their feelings toward Congress (remember the survey and the scandal both occurred in 1992): "There are many reasons people might have negative feelings toward Congress. I would like to know how much each of the following actions of Congress contribute to your negative feelings. Did the action contribute a great deal, some, a little, or not at all to your feelings? The overdrafts at the House bank."

The other question used to measure respondents' concern with members' ethics stems from answers to an open-ended question that queried respondents as to what they disliked about Congress. Respondents who reported that they disliked Congress because of unethical behavior were coded 2. Examples of such responses include "scandals," "corruption," "politicians not having values or principles," and "dishonesty in government." Respondents who gave vague responses that could indicate concern with ethics were given a value of 1. An example of a vague response is "member's behavior." "Member's behavior" may mean that members behave unethically or it may mean something else. Since the response was vague and potentially could involve ethics, it was included in this looser category. Responses that could not be interpreted to indicate unethical behavior as something a respondent disliked about Congress were coded 0.

An examination of these measures found that they were highly correlated and exhibited similar relationships with the dependent variables. They were combined into a summary measure that taps the respondent's concern with ethics. The two items used to create this measure were recoded so that each ranged from 0 to 1. Thus, the scale ranged from 0 to 2. To some readers this measure may appear to replicate the dependent variables: negative views about Congress. That is, both the summary measure of concern about ethics and the dependent variables assume that there is something to dislike about Congress. To control for this problem, respondents who failed to provide an answer to the open-ended question about what they disliked about Congress were omitted from the analysis.[11] Thus, this section examines whether respondents who were concerned with ethics violations in Congress have more negative feelings than people who were concerned with other problems in the institution.

To test whether respondents who were concerned about ethics had more negative feelings and attitudes toward Congress, OLS regression was used. Here, six control variables were included in the equations. One control variable was respondent's sex (men = 0 and women = 1). Another variable was respondent's level of education. Respondent's education was coded 1 to 8, with less than high school coded 1 and graduate degree coded 8. Hibbing and Theiss-Morse (1995) found that respondents' support for members and the institution varied across these categories, with women and those with lower levels of education tending to have higher levels of support. Another variable was respondent's political party (Democrats = 1, non-Democrats = 0). At the time of the survey, the Democratic Party controlled Congress; therefore, Democratic respondents may have been less concerned about the operations of Congress and the behavior of its members. Another control variable was respondent's external efficacy. It is expected that people who believe the government is responsive are less likely to be concerned about legislative ethics and more likely to support Congress.[12] Similarly, the respondent's interest in politics was controlled, since people who are interested in politics are likely to have a better idea of how Congress performs, which should affect their views of Congress.[13] Finally, knowledge about politics is likely to affect an understanding of Congressional ethics as well as of Congress itself. Knowledge was measured by correct responses to eight questions.[14]

Table 3.3 reports the means and standard deviations for each of the variables. The average feeling thermometer score for the membership was 42, and it was 66 for the institution. Similarly, the approval ratings for the membership were lower than for the institution (2 compared to 3). The average score for concern with ethics was .99, for political interest was 3.2, 1.38 for efficacy, 6.15 for knowledge, and 5.22 for education.[15] The average respondent was female and Republican.

The four dependent variables described earlier were regressed on the summary measure of concerns with ethics and the control variables. The results are presented in Table 3.4. Although the model explains little of the variance in the dependent variables, (note the small R^2s), the results show that respondents who reported that they were troubled by ethics in Congress were more likely to have negative views of both the members and the institution. It is important to note, however, that the influence unethical behaviors have on the public's perception was unevenly distributed between members and the insti-

Table 3.4
Concern for Ethics Effects on Feelings and Evaluations of Congress

	Feelings		Approval	
	Member	Institution	Member	Institution
Concern for Ethics	−10.89***	−4.97*	−.31***	−.04
	(1.99)	(2.74)	(.07)	(.07)
Interest	−1.79**	−2.76**	−.05*	.07***
	(.76)	(1.06)	(.03)	(.03)
Sex	3.21***	1.98	.09**	−.02
	(1.15)	(1.60)	(.04)	(.04)
Party	2.37*	.10	.11**	.04
	(1.27)	(1.76)	(.04)	(.04)
Efficacy	3.17***	3.20***	.10***	.08***
	(.56)	(.77)	(.02)	(.02)
Knowledge	−1.58***	.48	−.01	.02
	(.46)	(.64)	(.01)	(.02)
Education	.41	1.20***	−.02**	.03***
	(.31)	(.43)	(.01)	(.01)
Constant	56.57***	45.76***	2.36***	2.43***
R^2	.10	.06	.08	.07
n	917	930	897	925

Source: The data used here were collected in *Congress as Public Enemy: Public Attitudes toward American Political Institutions*, by J. R. Hibbing, and E. Theiss-Morse, 1995, New York: Cambridge University Press.

* <.10; ** <.05; *** <.01 (two-tailed test)

Key: Concern for ethics: combination score; see text (0 = not concerned with ethics; 2 = concerned with ethics)

Interest: 1 = not at all interested; 4 = very interested in politics

Sex: 0 = male; 1 = female

Party: 1 = Democrat; 0 = other

Efficacy: 0 = low efficacy; 3 = high efficacy

Knowledge: 0 = low knowledge; 8 = high knowledge

Education: 1 = less than high school; 8 = graduate degree

Feelings member: feeling thermometer about members

Feelings institution: feeling thermometer about institution

Approval member: 1 = strongly disapprove; 4 = strongly approve

Approval institution: 1 = strongly disapprove; 4 = strongly approve tution. Regardless of whether the feeling thermometer questions or the approval questions were examined, the public directed the balance of their negative attitudes toward members rather than the institution. The coefficient for "concern for ethics" effect on respondents' feelings toward the membership was −10.89, and was only −4.97 for the relationship between "concern for ethics" and feelings toward the institution. Similarly, the coefficient for "concern with ethics" effect on approval of the membership was −.31, and was only −.04 for "concern with ethics" effect on approval of the institution. This last relationship also failed to meet normal levels of statistical significance.

The effects of the control variables are noteworthy as well. Respondents who expressed an interest in politics had more negative feelings and lower approval ratings of the membership than those who were less interested in politics; however, the opposite was true for their approval of the institution. Women and Democrats had more positive feelings and approval ratings of the membership, but gender and party had little effect on attitudes toward the institution. Individuals with high levels of efficacy had more positive feelings and attitudes toward the membership and the institution than did others. Respondents' level of knowledge and education did not have consistent effects on their evaluations (feelings or approval) of Congress. Knowledge only significantly affected individuals' feelings toward the membership. The greater the knowledge, the less warmly respondents felt toward the membership, but knowledge had little effect on the other evaluations of Congress. While education generally had a positive effect on respondents' evaluation of Congress, it had a significant negative effect on approval of the membership.

The picture painted by the cross-sectional data fills in some of the broad stokes made by the earlier analysis. The analysis in this section indicates that while ethics violations lower the public's opinion of members of Congress and the institution, the effects on the institution did not reach normal levels of statistical significance. Thus, the system's legitimacy is not greatly jeopardized by ethics violations. Americans may not see the membership as ethical, but they see the system generally as ethical.

CONCLUSION

The goal of this chapter was to estimate how much effect the ethics reforms had on the accountability principle of Congress (i.e., the public's approval of Congress). To do this, two separate analyses were conducted. One examined the effects of news accounts of ethics violations on the public approval of Congress. The evidence from this analysis is that ethics violations cause a modest decline in approval ratings. It takes extensive news coverage of ethics violations for the coverage to have a noticeable effect on approval ratings, but sometimes the coverage is extensive. In addition, when Congress disciplines a member for unethical behavior it actually improves Congress's approval ratings, thereby recouping some of its loses in public approval caused by the ethics violations in the first place. A second analysis was conducted to see if ethics violations have a greater effect on Americans' attitudes and feelings toward Congress the institution or Congress the membership. This analysis indicated that ethics violations cause more harm to the public's feelings and evaluations of the membership of Congress than to their feelings and evaluations of the institution. That the public's reaction to the institution is only slightly affected by ethics violations implies that violations will not delegitimize Congress.

An assumption of this chapter was that the ethics reforms and climate would harm the public's confidence by increasing the number of ethics violations known to the public. Thus, in the initial analysis, reports of individual violations were examined to see the effects of these reports on public opinion. While this is a reasonable approach, there may be other ways the ethics reforms and climate could affect the public's attitudes. The reforms could alter Americans' expectations. We may have higher expectation of Congress and Congressional ethics because the media coverage and the rules tell Americans to expect ethical behavior on the part of members. Thus, the base level of approval or the importance of ethics in evaluations of Congress may have been altered. The reforms could also alter the atmosphere in Congress, which could affect approval ratings independent of specific violations. Americans do not like conflict, and the atmosphere in Congress during the ethics climate may be more conflictual, regardless of the number of allegations made against members, again altering the base of approval. At some level the later examination of the Hibbing and Theiss-Morse (1995) data offered a broader view, since a more general concern with ethics was examined. However, more research on the relationship between the ethics climate and public opinion is needed to fully test the effects of the ethics climate on Americans' feelings and evolutions of Congress.

So far this analysis of the effects of the ethics reforms on Congress suggest that by and large they have improved members' behavior and have not significantly decreased the public's support of Congress. It could still be that the ethics reforms have had other negative or positive consequences. The next chapter explores if the reforms may have improved ethics in Congress by removing members who violated the ethics standards and/or harm Congress by discouraging others from wanting to serve.

NOTES

1. Although some of the data in Chapter 2 did find that following the 1977 reforms the number of violations went down when compared to the period just before it, both periods were really part of the ethics climate that dates back to the 1960s. In addition, one can argue that the reforms increased the number of known cases because there were more House disciplinary actions against members following the reforms than prior to it.

2. Using quarterly data is very helpful in measuring approval ratings, and Stimson's measure has become widely accepted. However, it may minimize some of the effects of unethical behaviors, since it is not possible to determine if the ethics violation coverage preceded the surveys conducted in a quarter.

3. The author thanks R. H. Durr, J. B Gilmour, and C. Wolbrecht for letting her use their data.

4. The stories on Congressional ethics were found using the *New York Times* indices from 1973 to 1991. Stories discussing whether a member violated the ethics rule or the law were counted. These stories were found looking in the U.S. Congress section of the indices under the subheading of Ethics when it was available. For violations identified for the analyses in Chapters 4 through 6, stories were also found under the name of the members involved and other subheadings specific to the violation (e.g., House bank, Keating Five).

5. Since the *New York Times* was used I feared that the coverage would be biased toward New York–area members; that is, New York members' violations would receive greater coverage than other members' violations. However, there were relatively few violations that only involved a New York–area member. Analyses of the data indicate that including stories about New York members did not harm the detected relationship between news coverage of ethics violations and public approval. I also examined just front-page stories and stories that were classified as long by the *New York Times Index*, but an initial analysis of the data indicated that the number of stories had a stronger effect on approval ratings than did the other measures. Also, the number of stories was used by Patterson and Caldeira (1990) in their analysis.

6. Included in this measure were stories reporting that the ethics committee recommended a disciplinary action.

7. Regression is based on a linear equation where the slope (measured by the b coefficients) is the change in the dependent variable produced by a one-unit change in an independent variable. To estimate the public approval rating, the b coefficients can be multiplied by valid scores on the variables and added to the constant. The constant is the value of the dependent variable when the variables in the equation are zero. The R^2 indicates how much variance from the mean in the dependent variable is explained by the equation.

8. Three such variables were not used. Two were dichotomous measures of specific scandals. These variables were not needed, since a different measure of scandals was used. Also eliminated from the analysis was their measure of news tone. This variable overlaps to a large degree with my measure of scandals ($r = .53$).

9. Major bills passed was based on Mayhew's (1991) measure of major bills. It includes bills reported in end-of-session summaries in the *New York Times* and *Washington Post* and in books and articles written in later years that note the significance of a piece of legislation. Internal conflict was the number of cloture votes and debt ceiling bills. Expectation about the economy was the University of Michigan's Index of Consumer sentiment regressed on four indicators of the economy (see Durr et al., 1997, pp. 186–187).

10. The author thanks John Hibbing and Elizabeth Theiss-Morse for allowing her to use their data set.

11. A total of 1,265 respondents answered the open-ended question; 114 gave responses that were clearly related to unethical behavior and 173 gave responses that were either clearly or vaguely relating to unethical behavior.

12. Respondents were asked if they agreed with the following statements: "People like me don't have any say about what the government does. Voting is the only way people like me can have any say about how the government runs things. I don't think public officials care much about what people like me think." The responses range from low efficacy = 0 to high efficacy = 3.

13. This variable was measured by self-placement on a scale ranging from very interested = 4 to not interested at all = 1.

14. Respondents were asked who was head of Russia, who was secretary of state, and who was secretary of defense. They were also asked if the current (1992) budget deficit was larger or smaller when Reagan first entered office. They were also asked which party had the majority in the House and the Senate, how long a senator's term is, and how many senators are from the respondent's state. To minimize the number of missing cases, respondents who did not answer a question were assumed not to know the answer.

15. Since these are ordinal-level measures, the median may be preferred to the mean. The median for approval of the membership was 2 and 3 for the institution. The mean was 3 for concern of ethics, 3 for interest in politics, 1 for efficacy, 6 for knowledge, and 6 for education.

CHAPTER 4

The Effects of Ethics Standards
on Member Departure

After being convicted of ten federal charges of racketeering, bribery, tax evasion and fraud, Rep. James Traficant Jr. (D, OH) said he would not resign and
instead would run again as an independent.[1] However, members of both parties encouraged him to resign, and when he refused he became only the second person since the Civil War to be expelled. One of the potential values of
the ethics standards is that they may force out of office members whose behavior is egregious. Since the best predictor of future behavior is past behavior, if the ethics climate and reforms forced members who violated the standards
to leave office, they reduced the number of members likely to behave unethically.[2] Conversely, a potential negative side effect of the standards is that they
may simultaneously decrease the willingness of other members to serve. The
reforms increased the costs of service for all members by decreasing the ways
they can earn money, requiring financial disclosure, and perhaps increasing
the image of House members as unethical. These increased costs and decreased
benefits of House service likely make the job less desirable for other members. This chapter examines two ways the standards have affected members'
departure: causing members who have violated the rules to leave the chamber
and discouraging all members from wanting to serve.

DEPARTURE RATES OF THE ACCUSED

There are three ways that the ethics standards can remove members who
have behaved unethically: expulsion, lost reelection, and retirement.[3] How
successful these methods are in removing unethical members can be debated.
First let us look at expulsion. According to Article 1, Section 5 of the Constitution, "Each House may determine the Rules of its Proceedings, punish its

members for disorderly Behaviour, and, with the Concurrence of two thirds, expell a Member." The Constitution does not specify what types of offenses should result in expulsion, and the House has used this power infrequently. Besides Traficant only one representative has been expelled since the Civil War. Rep. Michael "Ozzie" Myers (D, PA) was expelled in 1980 on charges of corruption stemming from Abscam, an FBI sting operation. Rep. Myers was caught on videotape accepting $50,000 to introduce a private bill that would help a fictitious Arab gain residency in the United States.[4] There are other reasons why expulsion is not used more often. First, it requires a supermajority to expel a member, and provisions within the Constitution requiring a supermajority are rarely successful. A second reason is the system of self-discipline. As noted in Chapter 2, self-discipline makes conviction tough, since members do not like to serve as watchdogs of their peers. Also, members may resign from the House before the House acts.

Besides expulsion, ethics reforms can remove members who have violated the ethics standards through the ballot box. Elections were designed to force members to be accountable to their constituents. In part, that members know they must face reelection should force them to be good representatives, but it also serves as a way for voters to remove members who have violated their trust. The accountability function of elections is dependent on voters being able to remove members they dislike. If voters are not able to remove members who have violated their trust, then elections are no longer serving the accountability function.

Although voters clearly have the constitutional power to remove members who violate the ethics standards, voters cannot do so easily. Even if being accused of unethical behavior weakens incumbents, several factors can limit the ability of voters to replace unethical members. One factor is the incumbency advantage (Jacobson, 1997, chap. 3; Mayhew, 1974b). With incumbents winning by large margins, members can afford to lose a few thousand votes and still win reelection. Similarly, challengers tend to be underfunded and to lack political knowledge and name recognition. When the challenger is undesirable, voters may see it in their best interest to reelect an incumbent who may have violated their trust. Using experiments, Rundquist, Strom, and Peters (1977) found that while voters would not reelect an unethical member all things being equal, they would reelect a member who shares their issue preferences if the challenger does not. Thus, voters may vote for an unethical member because it is in their overall interest to do so. Although quality challengers may be inspired to run against an incumbent facing an allegation of unethical behavior, if the accusation was made late in a term, it may be too late for a quality challenger to emerge. In addition, since members build trust with their constituents, voters often want to believe their member's denial of wrongdoing.

Another factor that minimizes the effects of ethics violations on voters' decisions is that voters by and large have short attention spans. If the accusation is older than a few months, it is less likely to affect voters' candidate preferences than if it occurred closer to the election. The older the violation, the greater the opportunity voters have to forget or forgive the member for his or her transgression, or to get new information. Information voters receive after an ethics violation has been made public likely minimizes the effect of the violation on their vote (Alford, Teeters, Ward, & Wilson, 1994, p. 790).

Previous research that examines the effect of scandals on members' reelection bids presents a mixed picture. On one hand, Mondak (1995) and McCurley and Mondak (1995) found members' integrity related to their electoral prospects. Members having low levels of integrity were more likely to lose reelection than those with high levels of integrity. Thus, their research suggests that the electoral system is sensitive to members' ethics. On the other hand, examinations of the House banking scandal suggest that few members lost reelection because of the scandal (Alford et al., 1994; Banducci & Karp, 1994; but see Dimock & Jacobson, 1995; Jacobson & Dimock, 1994). Studies not limited to the House banking scandal also suggest a modest effect of scandals on reelection bids. In the 1960s and 1970s, Peters and Welch (1980) estimated a loss of 6 to 11 percent of the vote, while Welch and Hibbing (1997) estimated a 10 percent loss in vote during the 1980s. Since most incumbents are re-elected with greater than a 10 percent margin, ethical problems are not likely to cause many members to leave Congress through the ballot box.

The threat of expulsion, other punishments, or a fear of losing reelection can also cause members to retire. For example, Rep. John Jenrette (D, SC), who was stung in Abscam and lost reelection in November 1980, resigned before the House reconvened in December to vote on expelling him. Rep. Mario Biaggi (D, NY) resigned in 1988 after his second conviction of a felony, but before the House could vote to expel him. Having to face voters may also cause members who have been accused of unethical behavior to retire. If members feel they are likely to lose reelection because of an accusation, there is little value in committing to an exhausting reelection campaign. Members facing ethics charges may retire for other reasons as well. Speaker Jim Wright (D, TX) resigned in the middle of his term even though he had won a reelection bid after allegations became public and even though he was unlikely to have been expelled. Rep. Jon Hinson (R, MI) also resigned amid a sexual scandal for "the good of the party" shortly after being reelected ("Hinson Resignation," 1981, p. 385).

Examinations of the House banking scandal give us some indication of the effects of an accusation of unethical behavior on members' retirement. During the 1992 elections, the scandal was widely credited for causing a large number of retirements (Angle, 1992; Kuntz, 1992). Although seventy-seven of the members who bounced checks retired in 1992 ("Wave of Diversity," 1992, p. 17-A), scholars (Alford et al., 1994; Groseclose & Krehbiel, 1994; but see Banducci & Karp, 1994; Jacobson & Dimock, 1994) have been less optimistic about the effects of the scandal on retirements, citing other factors. The 1992 election was the first following redistricting, and 1992 was the last year members could pocket leftover campaign dollars upon retirement. Groseclose and Krehbiel (1994) estimated that once these other factors were considered, the scandal caused an increase of only about half a dozen retirements.

Since the effectiveness of expulsion, lost reelection, and retirement in removing unethical members is debatable, this section explores the overall survivability of members accused of violating ethics standards between 1977 and 2000. Members who faced either legal charges or were investigated by the Committee on the Standards of Official Conduct were considered to have been accused of violating the ethics standards. Several sources were used to identify such members between 1977 and 2000. *Congressional Quarterly's Almanac* (various years), *Congressional Ethics: History, Facts, and Controversy* (1992), and Thompson (1995) were examined for situations in which members were officially accused of either violating the House ethics standards or the law. From this information the names of individuals who faced allegations of wrongdoing were collected. For a list of the members accused of unethical behavior, see Appendix A. Of these members, only those who were accused of unethical behavior while still in office were examined. Members who had a series of violations were only examined following the first accusation, since it would be impossible to disentangle the effects of the different charges. Also, members who sought higher office following the accusation were not included in the study. This provided a list of ninety-nine members who could potentially be returned to office after being accused of unethical behavior.

Factors specific to a case may affect how long it takes for a member to retire or lose reelection following an accusation. A member who faces an accusation late in a term may be able to win the upcoming election only to have the investigation grow in the following years, face a tough challenge in the next election, and lose. Conversely, another member who had an issue brought up and resolved early in a term may be able to survive because of voters' short attention span. Because of this, the departure of members accused of unethical behavior was examined over two election cycles. Members leaving in the first election cycle were classified as having left in the short term and those leaving in the first or second election cycle were classified as leaving in the long term. For example, Rep. Earl Hilliard (D, AL), who was accused of misusing campaign funds in the 106th Congress and survived the 2000 elections but lost in 2002, was classified as not leaving in the short term but leaving in the long term. Had he lost in 2000 he would have been classified as leaving in the short term and the long term. One member, Dan Daniel (D, VA), was removed from the long-term analysis since he died in office after having survived in the short term.

An initial examination suggests that most members cannot survive an accusation of unethical behavior in the long term but can in the short term. Thirty-nine (39%) of the ninety-nine members left the House following the accusation. Although most members accused of unethical behavior remained in office, the departure rate for these members is much larger than that of other members. Between 1977 and 1999, the average turnover in an election year was 15 percent, with the 1992 election cycle resulting in the largest turnover, 25 percent. The departure rate for members accused of violating ethics in the long term is even higher. More than half (sixty-one members or 62%) of these members left within two election cycles of the accusation; therefore, most members accused of unethical behavior were gone from the House within four years of the accusation.

Both retirements and lost reelections contributed to this attrition. In the short term, electoral loss contributed to the greatest number of departures.[5] In the first election cycle, fourteen members (14%) retired instead of facing reelection and twenty-five members (25%) lost reelection. But in the second election cycle, retirements contributed more to departures, thirteen compared to nine. Thus, in the long term, electoral losses caused thirty-four departures and retirements caused twenty-seven.

If the standards are effective in removing unethical members, then members who caused the greatest harm to the legislative process should be more likely to leave the House than other members. Certainly members who were accused but found innocent of charges or received minor punishments should be less likely to leave than those found guilty of severe wrongdoing. Another way members' ethical violations may harm the legislative process is by violating the legislative principles of fairness, independence, and accountability. These were discussed in great detail in Chapters 1 and 2, but actions that give an undeserved advantage in the political or legislative sphere or prevent some members from fulfilling their obligations violate fairness, those preventing members from basing decisions on merit harm independence, and actions that harm the public's confidence in Congress harm accountability (Thompson, 1995).

To determine if members who cause the greatest harm to the legislative process were more likely to leave the House, two logistic regression equations were estimated. One examines whether members left in the short term and the other examines departures in the long term. Logistic regression was used instead of OLS regression, since the dependent variables were dichotomous: Members either leave or stay.[6] Logistic regression produces Maximum Likelihood Estimates (MLEs), which in this case estimate the logged odds that a member left. Since this figure is not easy to understand, the probabilities that members with particular characteristics leave are offered in Table 4.1 and discussed in the text. First I calculated the probability that the average member who had been accused of unethical behavior left. This was done by multiplying the MLE by the mean (rounded to the nearest whole number) for each variable, then adding these figures to the constant.[7] This figure is the Z. It is plugged into the following equation to estimate the probability that the average member was accused or convicted:

$$\text{Prob(leave)} = \frac{1}{1 + e^{-z}}$$

Table 4.1
Estimated Probabilities That Members with Specific Characteristics Leave

	Short term	Long term
Severity = 0	.47	.69
Severity = 1	.49	.73
Severity = 3	.56	.80
Resources = 0	.49	.73
Resources = 1	.29	.58
Principle = 0	.49	.73
Principle = 1	.44	.74
Media stories = 00	.41	.73
Media stories = 55	.49	.73
Media stories = 100	.56	.73
Leadership = 0	.49	.73
Leadership = 1	.04	.39
Previous vote = 50	.81	.89
Previous vote = 72	.49	.73
Previous vote = 90	.20	.51

Note: These were calculated assuming that all the characteristics, with the exception of the ones reported, were at the mean (rounded to the nearest whole number).

This probability is used as a base and then compared to the probabilities of members with a score different from the mean on one characteristic leave. These probabilities are calculated using the same formula.

Four variables were used to measure the harm that an activity caused the legislative process. First, in order to measure the harm a violation caused to the accountability principle, media coverage was used. In Chapter 3 the number of stories covering ethics violations was found to have at least some negative effects on the public's approval of the institution. Media coverage was measured by the number of stories in the *New York Times* that discussed the unethical behavior of a given member accused of violating the ethics standards or the law. These data were calculated for the period between the first report and the second election.

Another variable was used to measure whether or not the other legislative principles were harmed. Members who committed any of the following were considered to have violated independence: bribery, influence peddling, and receiving illegal gifts. Members who committed any of the following violations were considered to have harmed fairness: bribery, influence peddling, voter fraud, using their office for campaigning, and violating campaign finance law. Violations not considered to violate the legislative principles include drunkenness, drug use, sexual misconduct, using campaign or office for personal gain, tax fraud, or financial disclosure violations. Initial examinations indicated a strong correlation between whether members violated the fairness or independence principle (r = .76). Thus, they were combined into one variable, with members who violated either principle coded 1, and those who did not violate the principles coded 0.[8]

A third variable measured whether the ethics violation depleted legislative resources. Members who misused their offices, used staff for nonofficial work (including campaigning), or engaged in drug use in the capitol or sexual harassment involving Congressional staff were considered to have wasted resources and were coded 1.[9]

The final indicator of harm to the legislative process was the severity of the punishment dealt to the members. In theory, greater violations receive greater punishment than lesser violations do. For example, people who commit felonies get jail time and those committing misdemeanors are more likely to get fines, while people found innocent receive no punishment. To measure the severity of the offense, members who were not found to have violated the code of ethics or law were coded 0. Members who received letters of rebuke or were found to have violated the rules without the House acting were coded 1. For example, in the 100th Congress, Rep. Mary Rose Oakar (D, OH) was coded 1. She was investigated for paying a staff member who no longer worked on Capitol Hill. She was found to have violated the rules, but the committee recommended no disciplinary action except repayment of the payroll fund, which she had already done (*Congressional Ethics: History, Facts, and Controversy*, 1992, p. 77). Members who were reprimanded were coded 2. Members who were censured or found guilty of violating the law but did not receive a jail sentence were coded 3. Members who were expelled or jailed were coded 4. Since some members retired to avoid charges, members who retired after the House ethics committee recommended a sanction but before the House voted were coded as if the House voted for the recommended sanction.

In addition to these characteristics of members' offenses, several control variables were used.[10] First, members' electoral strength may affect members' survivability. The literature on Congressional retirements and reelection indicates that vulnerable members were more likely to leave (Frantzich, 1978; Hibbing, 1982; Kiewiet & Zeng, 1993; Jacobson, 1997; Welch & Hibbing, 1997). Candidates involved in scandals lose 5 to 10 percent of the vote on average (Peters & Welch, 1980; Welch & Hibbing, 1997); consequently a member who normally wins with 55 percent of the vote is more likely to be defeated than one who normally wins with 70 percent of the vote. Electorally vulnerable members also may be less likely to run for reelection, since running for reelection is difficult and expensive. If members feel the chance of reelection is remote, they might choose to retire. Electoral security was measured as the percentage of votes a member received in the election prior to the accusation. Percentage of vote is a common indicator of electoral marginality (Jacobson, 1997; Welch & Hibbing, 1997).

Another factor controlled for is institutional strength. Members who are powerful may be able to survive an allegation by preventing the committee or the House from sanctioning them. In testimony before the House Ethics Reform Task Force, Gary Ruskin, director of the Congressional Accountability Project, noted a number of incidences when the House Committee on Standards of Official Conduct stonewalled investigations of powerful members such as Majority Whip Tom Delay, and Transportation and Infrastructure Committee Chair Bud Shuster (U.S. House, 1997, pp. 98–100). Although he did not discuss this in terms of purposeful avoidance of the investigation of leaders, the cases he discussed indicated that the Committee on the Standards of Official Conduct is reluctant to fully investigate powerful members. Also, as will be discussed in Chapter 6, although leaders were more likely to be accused of violating the ethics standards than other members, they were less likely to be convicted.

There were two measures of institutional strength: leadership and party. Members holding any of the following positions were considered leaders: Speaker, majority and minority leaders, whips, and committee chairs. Members of the majority party may also be better able to survive an allegation, since the ethics process is often considered partisan (Getz, 1966, pp. 98–112; Thompson, 1995, pp. 146–150). Members of the majority party at the time of the accusation were coded 1 and others 0. Thus, prior to 1995, Democrats were coded 1 and following 1995 Republicans were coded 1.

Another control variable was the nature of the times. Over the twenty years studied, several changes took place in society that may have altered the survivability of members. The reforms were amended and improved over the twenty-five years studied. Thus, there were more rules to violate and a better infrastructure to prosecute cases later in the time period. Similarly, the media became more active in seeking out and reporting scandals (Garment, 1991; Lichter & Amundson, 1994; Robinson, 1994). Not only did the media become more likely to report on unethical behavior, but ethics charges have become "politics by other means." Ginsberg and Shefter (1990) argue that as the electoral process became less effective in choosing a single party to control the government, the parties fought in office by bringing charges of unethical behavior against each other. Increased awareness and partisan gamesmanship are likely to have lessened the effects of accusations of unethical behavior on members' departure. These political uses of ethics may have made it difficult for Americans to distinguish unethical behavior from unjustified accusations (Roberts & Doss, 1997). To see if there has been a decrease in the effects of accusations of unethical behavior on member departure, the year of the election following the allegation was used such that 1978 was coded 0, 1980 coded 1, 1982 coded 2, and so on.

Age is also likely to affect members' survivability. As with most jobs, older members are more likely to retire than younger members (Hibbing, 1982, p. 83). Being a member of Congress is often a stressful job and older members who are thinking of retiring may opt to retire when an accusation surfaces. Age was coded as members' age at the time of their first election following the accusation.

The data for the variables come from *Congressional Quarterly Almanacs, Congressional Quarterly Weekly Reports, Vital Statistics on Congress 1999–2000*, the *New York Times Index*, and the *Almanac of American Politics*. Tests for multicollinearity suggested that this was not a concern with these data. The means for the variables are listed in Table 4.2. On average, a member accused of an ethics violation received a very mild punishment, was of the

Table 4.2
Means and Standard Deviations for the Independent and Dependent Variables

	Means	S.D.	Short-Term r	Long-Term r
Left short term	.39	.49		
Left long term	.62	.49		
Severity of punishment	1.29	2.76	.06	.13
Resources	.22	.42	−.08	−.09
Principles	.43	.50	.00	.04
Media stories	55.15	85.39	.11	.07
Leadership	.30	.46	−.40***	−.21**
Majority party	.75	.44	−.05	.03
Previous vote	71.09	16.29	−.27***	−.23**
Year	5.98	3.22	−.09	−.11
Age	53.95	9.72	−.03	.03

Key: Severity: 4 = most severe; 0 = not found guilty of wrongdoing

Media: number of stories written about members' ethics violations

Leadership: 1 = held leadership position; 0 = did not hold leadership position

Majority party: 1 = majority party; 0 = minority party

Principles: 1 = violated fairness or independence principle; 0 = principles not violated

Previous vote: percentage of vote member received in their last election

Year: year of election following accusation, such that 1978 = 1, 1980 = 2, and so on

Age: member's age during election immediately following accusation

Resources: 1 = ethics violation involved loss of resources; 0 = otherwise

*< .10; **< .05; ***< .01 (using two-tailed test)

majority party but was not a leader, was fifty-four years old, and received 71 percent of the vote in the election prior to the accusation.[11] The average member's violation did not harm the independence or fairness principle, or deplete legislative resources. The average accusation occurred in 1990 and had fifty-five stories about it in the *New York Times*.[12]

Table 4.2 also presents the bivariate correlations between each of the factors thought to increase the odds that members left the House and whether they left in the long or short term. The bivariate correlations suggest that the characteristics of the allegations had little effect on which members left. The type of punishment, the number of news stories, and whether the violation harmed the legislative principles or misused legislative resources did not have significant effects on whether a member left in the long or short term. And to the degree that misusing resources had any effect it decreased the chance that a member left the House. Instead, the main factors correlated to which members left were having a leadership position and electoral security.

Table 4.3 indicates that the model did a nice job predicting which members accused of unethical behavior left office. In the long term, it accurately predicted 71 percent of the cases; this is a 10-percent improvement over predicting the mean and in the short term it accurately predicted 81 percent of the cases for a 20-percent improvement.[13] Consistent with the bivariate findings, the model provides only modest evidence that members who harmed the legislative process were more likely to leave than those whose violations were more benign. The data suggest, in fact, that members who used resources or violated the principles of fairness and independence were slightly less likely to leave. This is evident because the MLE estimate is negative. However, the strength of the relationships was weak, not meeting normal levels of statistical significance.[14] This is true in the short and the long term. Even if media coverage is related to the accountability principle, members causing the greatest harm to accountability were not significantly more likely to leave than others. Although the direction of the relationship suggests that the more coverage members' accusations received the more likely they were to leave, the relationship was not statistically or substantively strong. The only evidence that members who caused the greatest harm left is that the stronger the punishment, the more likely members were to leave. However, only in the long term did the severity of the punishment meet the normal level of statistical significance.

Although the severity of the punishment was related to members' departures, the strength of its effect on departure rates pales in comparison to the effects of electoral security on members' survivability. Previous vote total clearly had the strongest effect on the departure rates of unethical members. Members who were electorally weak were significantly more likely to leave after an accusation was made against them. Even members who arguably violate their constituents' trust and harm the legislative process can be returned to office if they come from a safe district. The ability of the current system to remove unethical members was also hampered by members' institutional power.

Table 4.3
Logistic Regression for Departures

	Short Term		Long Term	
	MLE	S.E.	MLE	S.E.
Resources	−.85	.64	−.68	.60
Principles	−.20	.58	.04	.53
Severity	.15	.10	.18	.10*
Media	.006	.004	.000	.004
Previous vote	−.07	.02***	−.05	.02***
Leadership	−3.10	.75***	−1.43	.52**
Party	−.22	.61	.23	.55
Year	.09	.10	−.01	.09
Age	.01	.03	.03	.03
Constant	3.59	1.80**	2.58	1.66
Frequency of dependent variables				
Survived	.61		.38	
Departed	.39		.62	
Proportion correct				
Total	.81		.71	
Survived	.85		.54	
Left	.74		.82	
Proportion reduction in error	.20		.10	
Model chi-square	37.45		18.41	
Probability (chi-square)	.00		.03	
N	99		98	

$*< .10; **< .05; ***< .01$ (using two-tailed test)

Leaders were significantly less likely to leave in the short and the long term than were other members.

The other control variables only had modest effects on survivability. Although members who were accused in more recent Congresses and those who were older were more likely to leave, the coefficients were quite small and did not meet normal levels of statistical significance. The effect of majority-party status on members' survivability also was not significant and the direction of the relationship was negative in the short term and positive in the long term.

To help demonstrate the strength of the influence of the variables on the likelihood members leave, Table 4.1 presents the probabilities that members with different characteristics leave. As noted earlier, members who misused resources and violated the principles were modestly less likely to leave than other members were. The probability that a member who misused legislative resources left in the short term was .29, while it was .49 for a member who did not. In the long term the differences were .58 and .73, respectively. The probability that a member who violated either the fairness or independence principle left in the short term was .44 compared to .49 for a member who did not violate a principle. In the long term the difference was even smaller, at .74 to .73, respectively. Likewise, the change in the probability based on the number of media stories was moderately small, but here the direction does suggest that members causing greater harm were more likely to leave. In the short term the probability that a member who had no stories written about the accusation leaving was .41, while it was .56 for a member with 100 stories. In the long term the probability was the same regardless of the number of stories (.73). The severity of the punishment had a larger effect. The probability that a member who did not receive a punishment left in the short term was .47, compared to a probability of .56 for a member who was censured. For the long term the probabilities were .69 and .80, respectively.

Just as the sample probabilities can demonstrate the minimal importance of the characteristics of the accusation on whether a member leaves, the samples can demonstrate the importance of holding a leadership position and electoral security. While the probability that a rank-and-file member accused of violating the ethics standards left was .49 in the short term and .73 in the long term, for a leader the probabilities were .04 and .39, respectively. Similarly, while the probability that a member who faced a tough reelection bid prior to the accusation was high, it was low for those who had an easy victory. For a member winning with 50 percent of the vote, the probability of leaving was .81 in the short term and .89 in the long term, while the probabilities for a member who won with 90 percent of the vote were .20 and .51, respectively. These probabilities not only demonstrate the importance of electoral strength, but also indicate that the effects of electoral security were strongest in the short term. The difference in the probability of returning between those winning the previous election with 90 or 50 percent of the vote was .61 in the short term and .38 in the long term.

These findings give a mixed impression of the ability of the ethics reforms to remove members who harmed the legislative process. On one hand, the more severe members' punishments, the more likely they were to leave office, and there was some weak evidence that accused members who violated the accountability principle were more likely to leave than others. On the other hand, whether the accusation affected the fairness or independence principles or depleted legislative resources had virtually no effect on whether members accused of unethical behavior left office, and to the degree it did it decreased the odds they would leave. Also, whether a member was a leader or not or came from a safe or marginal district had the greatest effect on whether accused members left the House. That the competitiveness of members' districts has the largest effect on which members accused of unethical behavior leave shows a value to having competitive districts. They help insure ethical members are in Congress. Competitive districts are likely to encourage quality challengers to run against members who violate ethics standards and thus are likely to give voters an option to vote against a member who behaves unethically.

EFFECTS ON ALL MEMBERS

In addition to the effects that the ethics reforms had on the departure rate of members accused of unethical behavior, the heightened ethical standards may have decreased the value of service for ethical members and decreased their willingness to serve. During debate on the 1977 ethics reforms, Rep. Robert McClory (R, IL) expressed the fear that the reforms would discourage some Americans from running for Congress:

But I think that before adopting it [outside earnings limits] the House should consider whether it will discourage in the process many talented future Members. . . . I think—as to whether the infringements on personal privacy that the new code of ethics entails will discourage people of substance from careers in the House.

Certainly, the earnings limitation will have that effect. What this provision will bring us is a membership of two kinds of people. The very rich, whose so-called unearned income is not limited, and those who depend on the recently adjusted Congressional salaries for their livelihood. . . . And who are we discouraging from running?

Successful men and women from business and the professions, whose performance in private life indicates their understanding of the American system of government, and their belief in its values. (*Cong. Rec.*, 1977, p. 5922)

If members are assumed to be rational actors who will serve if the value of the job exceeds the costs, then there are several ways in which enhanced ethics may decrease the willingness of people to serve by increasing the costs and decreasing the benefits.

First, enhanced ethics standards have increased the cost of service for members. The rules have taken away members' ability to earn money. For example, members are limited in earning income outside of Congress, and prohibited from working in a law firm. While these rules limit potential problems with members dividing their attention between their profession and Congress and with other conflicts of interest, they also limit members' ability to earn larger incomes. The rules prohibiting members from receiving honoraria also decrease the material rewards of service. Prior to the ban on members keeping honoraria, some members earned several thousand dollars a year giving speeches. Again, there are justifications for the ban, but nevertheless, it limits the value of the job to members wanting or needing extra money. Thus, members can make less money today than in the past. This loss of revenue is a concern of many members. Former Rep. Robert Livingston (R, LA) complained about his inability to make money while in office, and considered retiring in order to earn more (Katz, 1998, p. 979).

In order to estimate the effects of the reforms on members' satisfaction with the job, the survey described in Chapter 2 also included questions about how the ethics reforms increased the costs of service. Of the thirty-nine former members interviewed, seventeen mentioned the loss of income either due to outside earning limits, stock losses, or honoraria as a personal cost of the reforms. One member said, "The loss of outside income was very tough on me. I earned $80,000 in 1974 as a lawyer (before Congress). In 1975 as a Congressman my salary was $42,500—plus I had to personally pay for a second home in Washington, D.C." Another member noted when he sold some stock he had to take a tax loss. Another member said, "My hunch is that the so called 'reforms', taken as a whole, have made it harder to serve except for those with outside incomes. It would be interesting to study whether the number of members of independent means has changed much over the years."[15] Another member said, "The upkeep of two homes (in DC and one's Congressional District) is costly. Add that to the education of one's children and the salary doesn't quite cover. Therefore, many members gave up their offices so that they could . . . earn sufficient funds to meet their family obligations."

The reforms may have additional costs for members who have careers that are hard to leave for a few years. For example, the House ethics committee ruled that doctors could not earn outside incomes. Rep. Tom Coburn (R, OK), who is a medical doctor, claimed that the decision is detrimental to medical doctors who want to serve in Congress because it forces them to choose between remaining active in their profession and serving in Congress. Doctors need to practice their profession to keep up to date and they need to charge to do this so that they can pay for insurance, nursing staff, and the like. He further worried that similar rulings will discourage citizen legislators. At one point he even threatened to leave the House over this issue. The issue was resolved to Coburn's satisfaction and he remained in the House until his self-imposed term limit was up (Peaden & Herrick, 2001).

The rules have increased other costs of service as well. Members have to learn the rules. The rules are intricate and often confusing if not carefully studied. If members make even an honest mistake, there are costs to their reputations, families, and finances. To avoid mistakes, members often ask for advisory opinions, which also absorbs members' time. One former member wrote that he had a friend who was a well-known painter, but before he could accept a painting from his friend he felt compelled to check with the ethics committee.

Another cost expressed by some members included the time and money spent filling out the financial disclosure forms. One member complained of the hours spent preparing the forms and another of personally paying for an accountant. In addition, one member blamed the disclosure forms for a series of break-ins at members' homes: "After disclosure, many homes of Congressmen, including mine, were broken into. Our loses were not substantial—ancestors' wedding ring, silver, etc., but we know where the thief got his prospective list."

Another way the increased focus on ethics has harmed the value of Congressional service is by focusing American's attention on the "bad apples." One value of serving in Congress is the prestige and honor members are rewarded for serving their country. However, the focus on ethics has undoubtedly decreased that value. Chapter 3 demonstrated that news coverage of ethics violations decreased American's affection for and evaluation of members of Congress. Thus, not only did the focus on ethics decrease the financial value of the job, but it also decreased the psychological value of the job.

Proving that the standards have caused members to leave is difficult. Too much changed at the same time as the ethics reforms to do a time series analysis. Congress went through a variety of reforms during the 1970s. Nevertheless, there is some circumstantial evidence that turnover has increased due to heightened concern with ethics. First, the evidence demonstrates that many members found the reforms decreased their enjoyment of the job or their job satisfaction. Job satisfaction increases when individuals' goals or values are met (Locke, 1983). By decreasing members' ability to meet their financial goals, as well as their time to meet other goals, the reforms undoubtedly decreased members' job satisfaction. Job satisfaction has been found elsewhere to be related to career length or members' willingness to serve (Fisher & Herrick, 2002).

Second, there tends to be larger turnover in House elections following major scandals. In 1974, following Watergate, which did not directly involve Congress, 102 members left. Following the House banking scandal in 1992, there was turnover of 120 members. Following Koreagate, 77 members left, and following Abscam, 74 left. These figures are higher than the average election-year turnover from 1974 to 1999 of 67. While some of the turnover in these elections was caused by members involved in scandals leaving, the difference in turnover between years with accusations of unethical behavior and those without is usually larger than the number of members leaving who were involved in a scandal. Similarly, the number of members who have served over ten years has declined since the 1970s. From the 91st to the 95th Congress about 17 percent of the members had served ten years or more. From the 96th through the 106th Congress, about 14 percent of the members served more than ten years (Ornstein, Mann, & Malbin, 2000).

There are also examples of members who committed no violations who left or almost left because of the ethics climate. As noted, Rep. Coburn threatened to retire in order to keep his medical practice. In an interview with Hibbing in 1978, one member said, "People just presume we are dishonorable. I don't know if you have ever been suspected of doing something dishonest, but if you have you know it is not a pleasant feeling until you are cleared. Well imagine living under a cloud of suspicion all the time. If you can do that, you can understand why some of us think serving in Congress isn't enjoyable" (Hibbing, 1982, p. 55). Other members who did not claim ethics rules encouraged their retirements did note that the disclosure rules were embarrassing and unfair, while others complained about investigations and hostile news reports (pp. 50–53).

CONCLUSION

The combination of expulsion, retirement, and lost reelection resulted in 39 percent of the members accused of ethical violations leaving the House during the Congress of the initial accusation, and 62 percent within two Congresses of the accusation. On the surface, this indicates one value to the ethics reforms: removal of unethical members. The value of the reforms in this regard, however, may be limited if it is not the members causing the greatest harm that leave.

While the results suggest that members who caused the greatest harm to the accountability principle and who received the stiffest punishment were at least modestly more likely to leave than others, those who depleted legislative resources and harmed the independence and fairness principles were not less likely to leave than members committing other types of violations. Also, members' electoral security and institutional power, not type of violation, had the strongest effects on the survivability of members accused of unethical behavior. Members who had been accused of unethical behavior and who easily won the previous election or held leadership positions were better able to withstand the allegations and return to Congress than were other members accused of wrongdoing. These findings suggest a need to improve the competitiveness of elections, and will be discussed in more detail in the concluding chapter.

Members violating the ethics standards are not the only members to leave because of the standards. This chapter also provided evidence that the standards made the job less attractive for all members. Although no hard evidence of a massive exodus from the House because of the standards was found, there was circumstantial evidence. Members complained about the added burdens of the standards, some are known to have contemplated retirement because of it, and the retention of members has declined as the reforms have gone into effect.

In sum, the heightened ethics standards have been relatively effective at removing members accused of unethical behavior, but their effectiveness is incomplete. Members who cause the greatest harm to the legislative process are not necessarily the most likely to leave. In addition, some members found the new standards to have increased the costs of service, and the new standards may have encouraged some to retire. Ways to improve the process to deal with these problems will be addressed in the concluding chapter. The next chapter explores whether the reforms increased the difficulty Congress has in enacting legislation.

NOTES

1. This chapter is based on Herrick (2000). The author thanks Sage Publications for permission to reprint part of this work.

2. In fact, members who have been accused once are more likely to be accused a second time than other members are to ever be accused (see Chapter 2). As with the analysis in Chapter 3, a key assumption with this chapter is that the reforms and climate had certain effects because they increased the visibility or known cases of unethical behavior. Thus, by identifying members who behave unethically the House can help remove these members. There are undoubtedly other ways the reforms may affect the willingness of unethical politicians to serve. For example, potential members inclined to violate ethics may simply chose not to seek office in the first place. Measuring the occurrence of such a phenomenon, however, is virtually impossible.

3. While "resign" indicates leaving during the term and "retire" means not seeking reelection, I use the terms interchangeably. This is done since it is not easy, nor necessary, to distinguish between the two. Members may resign late in the term to allow a new member to have extra seniority after they had already announced their retirement. Also, a few members resigned after they lost their reelection. Thus, the meaning of resigning is not always clear.

4. While expulsion removes a member from office, it does not prevent members from running for the House again. After being expelled, Myers ran for his old seat. Although he won the primary, he only garnered 38 percent of the vote in the general election. Thus, expulsion was effective in removing him.

5. Both Reps. Traficant and Myers, who were expelled, were coded as losing reelection since they tried unsuccessfully to run for their seats after expulsion. Had they been removed from the analysis, electoral loss would still be the main cause for members leaving.

6. Logistic regression is preferred to the easier to interpret and more common OLS regression. With OLS the estimation is linear. However, with a dichotomous dependent variable a linear equation is not possible because a score of greater than 1 or less than 0 is possible. Logistic regression, therefore, is based on an "S" curve so that no estimated value of the dependent variable is greater than 1 or less than 0.

7. The constant is the logged odd of being accused (or convicted) when all the other variables are 0.

8. My conceptualization of what it takes to violate these principles is much softer than that used by Thompson (1995). For example, Thompson suggests that to violate the independence principle members' behavior must actually be altered by something like a gift. Since proving that members were actually affected by the gifts would involve an investigation of the member's intentions, it would be virtually impossible to prove.

9. Drug use is considered a lost resource because members acting under the influence are unlikely to function at their highest level. Sexual harassment of employees also makes it more difficult for them to perform well. Drug use and sexual misconduct occurring off of Capitol Hill, however, were not included because they are less likely to involve legislative resources.

10. I also examined race to see whether white or African-American members were more likely to survive accusations of unethical behavior. However, the correlations between race and leaving the House after an accusation were small and not statisti-

cally significant. In the short term the correlation was .07 (p = .47), and in the long term it was .05 (p = .50). Since the theoretical argument to expect such a difference is difficult to make, these results are not reported or discussed.

11. Since this measure is ordinal I also report the median. It was 0.

12. This number is somewhat high because the accusations receiving the most stories involved multiple members. For example, twenty-two members were cited as violating the House bank and there were seventy-nine stories about the House bank scandal.

13. Some scholars question the value of looking at the ability of the model to accurately predict the dependent variable. This is because the dependent variable is dichotomous and the formula to predict the outcome rounds up. For example, if a member's score was .51, he or she would be predicted to leave, but if it was .49, he or she would be predicted not to leave. So even though the scores are very close, one case would be completely right and the other would be completely wrong.

14. Since the data set includes the entire population and not a sample, the value of measures of statistical significance is debatable. I report the level of statistical significance for those who find them helpful.

15. I examined correlations between members' wealth and the year they entered Congress. The correlations were positive and statistically significant (r = .13, p = .00), indicating that members today are wealthier than members in the 1970s. See Chapter 6 for a discussion of how wealth was measured.

CHAPTER 5

The Ethics Reforms and Lawmaking

The ethics climate undoubtedly increased the number of investigations of unethical behavior conducted by the House.[1] What is less clear is the degree to which the investigations made legislating difficult for Congress. It seems likely that investigations divert legislative resources away from legislating, for the accused as well as the other members. When the House votes to punish or investigate a member it is not spending its time making policy or representing the interests salient to the people. Investigations may increase the difficulty in building coalitions needed to pass legislation if they increase acrimony and partisanship. In addition, Congress will lose the work of those members who have been accused. Their attention will be diverted from representing their constituents and making laws to defending themselves. This chapter reports on two analyses to determine the extent to which the heightened ethics standards have limited Congress's and its members' ability to fulfill their legislative functions. First, it explores whether during the course of investigations Congress is less able to pass legislation than at other times. Second, the chapter examines how accusations of unethical behavior affect the ability of those accused to perform their duties.

HOW ETHICS VIOLATIONS MAY HARM LAWMAKING

There are two ways ethics investigations can decrease Congress's ability to pass laws: decreased time available and increased acrimony. Time is critical to policy making. The longest life a bill can have is two years, as bills die if they do not pass during a Congress. Consequently, at the end of every Congress several key pieces of legislation die without coming to a final vote. For example, the 103rd Congress ended without finishing its work on campaign finance, lobbying disclosure, telecommunications, and toxic waste (Cloud, 1994a). While time is not the only factor that prevents completion of legislation, it is a critical one. Legislative time is limited, and anything that diverts floor time from legislating reduces the odds of any one piece of legislation passing. In addition, increased time demands on Congress can cause conflicts between legislative goals (Connor & Oppenheimer, 1993). Congress is expected to do much by the public and by Constitutional obligations. It is expected to oversee the bureaucracy, to pass intelligently constructed legislation, and to represent each district as well as the nation as a whole. While these are not necessarily mutually exclusive activities, when time is limited one goal can get in the way of another. For example, how should Congress allocate its time between legislating or overseeing the bureaucracy? If there were no time constraints, Congress could do both, but as time constraints increase, the decision on which to do becomes tougher.

Time would not be an issue if Congress was not constitutionally constrained to a two-year window for considering legislation or if the numbers of bills for consideration were small. Earlier Congresses had the luxury of a limited legislative agenda. However, Congress's workload in the later half of the twentieth and the beginning of the twenty-first centuries is such that time has become a limited resource. The number of hours of debate in the House per term has risen from 1,332 for the 86th to 90th Congresses, to 1,643 hours for the 91st to 95th, to 1,691 for the 96th to 100th, and 1,963 hours for the 101st to 105th Congresses (Ornstein, Mann, & Malbin, 2000). In addition, members complain about the scheduling of floor debates and a generally chaotic work environment. Because of the time constraints, any time consumed by debating questions of ethical misbehavior decreases the likelihood that any given bill will be debated.

An additional way that ethics violations and investigations can harm the legislative process is by destroying the civility of debates and lessening members' ability to forge coalitions. Ethics investigations in Congress tend to dissolve into partisan battles, with Democrats defending Democrats and accusing Republicans and Republicans defending Republicans and accusing Democrats. As discussed in earlier chapters, attacking the other side's ethics has become politics by other means: a way to try to continue election battles when no side clearly wins. The increased partisanship and attendant decline in civility may decrease Congress's ability to pass legislation in a closely divided chamber where bipartisan cooperation is needed.

DO INVESTIGATIONS LIMIT CONGRESS'S ABILITY TO PASS LEGISLATION?

To determine if ethics investigations limit Congress's ability to pass legislation, the relationship between news coverage of violations and the ability to pass legislation will be estimated. To measure Congress's ability to pass legislation the number of bills passed and the number of major bills passed during each quarter from 1974 to 1994 were used.[2] The data for both of these variables come from Durr, Gilmour, and Wolbrecht (1997). They used Mayhew's (1991) figures for major bills passed.[3] These serve as dependent variables. To measure the existence of ethics investigations I used the measure of *New York Times* coverage of ethics violations used in Chapter 3. Other possible indicators of ethics investigations could include the number of resolutions to discipline a member that were debated and the amount of floor or committee time spent on an investigation. These indicators would have the advantage of appearing to be direct indicators of actions directly diverting legislative time. However, they only measure official formal investigations and debate, and the investigations could have effects on the legislative process beyond the formal stages. For example, the House never voted to sanction Rep. Daniel Rostenkowski after his conviction in the 103rd Congress. Yet the loss of the Ways and Means Committee chair likely affected policy making. As noted, the political use of ethics can change the environment of Congress, increasing acrimony and conflict. In addition, much work on ethics investigations could be done behind the scenes, or even in a year or Congress prior to the votes on the floor. For example, Newt Gingrich's reprimand occurred in the 105th Congress even though much of the official and unofficial debate occurred in the 104th. Thus, I chose to examine media coverage as an indicator of the overall significance of the violation, assuming it was related to the effects of the investigations inside of Congress.[4]

Since other factors can affect the relationship between ethics violations and Congress's ability to pass legislation, several control variables were used. The control variables were whether it was an election year, number of vetoes, number of overrides, institutional conflict, economic expectations, the year, and the quarter in the year (see Chapter 3 for discussion of the operational definitions of veto, override, institutional conflict, economic expectations, and year). Quarter was coded such that the first quarter in a year (January through March) was coded 1, the second quarter (April through June) was coded 2, and so on. Election year was coded such that election years were coded 1 and nonelection years coded 0. Generally, Congress is expected to pass more bills during election years (although it is not expected to pass more major bills in election years), late in the year, when there is less conflict between the institutions, and when economic expectations are high.[5] To control for these variables, OLS regression was used.[6] The effects of ethics violations on legislating were tested with the two dependent variables: number of bills passed and number of major bills passed.

The results of two regression analyses are reported in Table 5.1. The first column examines the number of total bills passed. It indicated that, overall, the model performed well. The R^2 was .85 and most of the control variables were statistically significant. The fewer number of overrides and the less internal conflict, the more bills passed. In election years and late in the year

Table 5.1
The Effects of Ethics Violations on the Passage of Bills and the Passage of Major Bills

	Bills Passed		Major Bills Passed	
	b	S.E.	b	S.E.
Scandal stories	.10	(.20)	−.0027	(.009)
Vetoes	4.16	(.88)***	.09	(.037)**
Overrides	−12.57	(5.13)**	.33	(.22)
Economic expectations	.04	(.28)	−.01	(.01)
Internal conflict	−2.30	(1.04)**	−.02	(.05)
Election year	33.62	(6.94)***	.16	(.30)
Quarter	39.03	(3.23)***	.55	(.14)***
Year	.85	(.63)	.03	(.03)
Constant	−56.45	(23.01)**	.18	(1.00)
R^2	.85		.49	
N	80		80	

Source: Much of the data used here were taken from "Explaining Congressional Approval," by R. H. Durr, J. B. Gilmour, and C. Wolbrecht, 1997, *American Journal of Political Science, 41*, pp. 75–207.

Note: Numbers in parentheses are standard errors.

*< .10; **< .05; ***< .01 (using two-tailed test)

Congress also passed more bills. Unexpectedly, though, the more vetoes that occurred in a quarter, the more bills passed, and the more overrides, the fewer bills passed. One explanation for this is that bill frequency increases the number of opportunities presidents have to veto bills (Copeland, 1983). Only two of the control variables, public's economic expectations and the year, did not have significant effects on the number of bills Congress was able to pass. Most relevant to this project, though, is the effects of ethics violations on the number of bills passed. These findings indicate that Congress was actually able to pass more, not fewer, bills as the number of news stories covering ethics violations rose. For every story on an ethics violation, .10 more bills passed. However, the relationship was not statistically significant (p = .61).[7]

The second column, which looks at passage of major bills, also provides very little evidence that investigations of violations harm Congress's ability to pass legislation. For every story on a Congressional ethics violation in the *New York Times* there were .0027 fewer major bills passed. Thus, even in the quarter with sixty-one stories the model predicts that Congress would pass about .16 fewer major bills. The relationship was not only substantively small, it was not statistically significant (p = .76). This model, however, did a fairly nice job predicting the number of major bills passed (R^2 = .49). However, two of the control variables accounted for the bulk of the model's ability to predict: the quarter and the number of vetoes. None of the other variables had statistically significant effects on the number of major bills Congress was able to pass.

This model assumes that the effects of the reports of unethical behavior would be felt immediately. However, it may be that there is a delay between the reports of unethical behavior and a decline in lawmaking. Initial reports that a problem occurs may not engage the membership, but as members have to make decisions on their colleagues, time is diverted and conflict increases. Also, if the investigation of unethical behavior creates an acrimonious environment, the negative effects of the unethical behavior may persist after the investigation is completed. Because it is possible that there could be a lagged effect of the investigations, the regression equations were rerun using the stories from the previous quarter. These findings are reported in Table 5.2. The

Table 5.2
The Effects of Ethics Violations on the Passage of Bills and the Passage of Major Bills, Lagged Effect

	Bills Passed		Major Bills Passed	
	b	S.E.	b	S.E.
Scandal stories(t-1)	−.40	(.20)**	−.0001	(.009)
Economic expectations	−.14	(.28)	−.01	(.01)
Vetoes	3.85	(.86)***	.09	(.04)**
Overrides	−12.60	(5.02)**	.34	(.22)
Institutional conflict	−2.73	(1.03)***	−.02	(.05)
Election year	36.29	(6.80)***	.12	(.30)
Quarter	39.89	(3.22)***	.56	(.14)***
Year	.89	(.63)	.03	(.03)
Constant	−33.87	(22.82)***	.05	(1.02)
R^2	.85		.50	
N	79		79	

Source: Much of the data used here were taken from "Explaining Congressional Approval," by R. H. Durr, J. B. Gilmour, and C Wolbrecht, 1997, *American Journal of Political Science, 41*, pp. 75–207.

Note: Numbers in parentheses are standard errors.

*< .10; **< .05; ***< .01 (using two-tailed test)

relationship between news accounts of ethical violations and major bills passed remained very small (b −.0009 and p = .92). However, the relationship for total bills passed changed directions and became statistically significant. For every news account in the previous quarter there were .4 fewer bills passed. What this suggests is that while the ethics investigations have little effect on the number of major bills passed, there are lingering effects on the overall ability of Congress to pass legislation. Since there is a lagged effect it may not be the time spent on the floor debating bills that harms the process but the lingering effects on the environment more generally. I calculated the number of resolutions dealing with ethics violations and the number of votes cast dealing with these House resolutions to gauge how much time is really spent on investigating ethics violations on the floor.[8] The House averaged fewer than four resolutions in a Congress and five votes.

Investigating members' ethics may also have subtle effects on the ability of Congress to legislate that were not detected here. It is possible that ethics violations increase the need for behind-the-scenes persuasion and arm twisting. As a consequence, debates may become acrimonious and the resulting bills may differ from those that would have passed without the violations. However, tests of these effects are virtually impossible.

THE ACCUSED AND LAWMAKING

Although ethics investigations only have a modest effect on Congress's ability to make laws, members who have been accused may have a hard time fulfilling their responsibilities as lawmakers. Members accused of unethical behavior are very likely to be profoundly affected by the experience and change their legislative styles as a result. This section examines whether being charged with ethics violations reduces members' legislative work. Specifically, it examines whether being accused of unethical behavior lessens members' activity and legislative effectiveness.

Accusing members of unethical behavior may affect these members' ability to represent their constituents and to legislate.[9] Members may be required to devote so much time and energy to defending themselves that they cannot be effective representatives or legislators. They may be visiting with attorneys, attending meetings in reference to the accusations, looking at their documents, or even spending time on trial. For example, it is unlikely that while Rep. Traficant spent two-and-a-half months serving as his own attorney in his trial that he had much time for working on legislation. One way to measure whether accusations divert members' attention is to look for a decline in their legislative activity. Members accused of ethics violations are likely to be diverted from legislative responsibilities by the need to spend time defending themselves. In an environment where members are already overbooked, members accused of unethical behavior are likely to face a choice between defending themselves or continuing to be devoted to their legislative and constituent work.

In addition to limiting levels of activity, being accused of unethical behavior also may affect members' ability to be effective legislators. Being able to shepherd legislation through the process not only indicates that a member has the knowledge and skill needed, but also that other members are willing to support the member's efforts. It is likely that when members are investigated, their effectiveness diminishes. Politics is a game of bargaining and deal making. In order to make deals, members have to be trusted. Since members being investigated may be seen as less trustworthy than others, they may lose some of their bargaining leverage. In addition, passing legislation takes time and energy, and as noted earlier, members defending themselves against accusations of unethical behavior may not have enough time to work on their legislative agenda.

To estimate the effect that being accused has on members' legislative behavior, I examined members who were accused of violating House rules or the law between 1977 and 2000. For information on how these cases were identified, see Chapter 4. Members who resigned or retired from the House while they faced charges were not examined, since the decision to retire alters members' behavior (Herrick, Moore, & Hibbing, 1994). Members who lost their reelection bids, however, were included, since they were not lame ducks until after the election. In addition, members who had multiple accusations were only examined at the time of the first charge. This was done because it would be impossible to separate the effects of the first from the second accusation for those with an ongoing investigation or a series of accusations. Also removed were House Speakers, since they do not participate in roll-call votes, and freshmen members, since they do not have a record of legislative activity prior to the accusation. This leaves seventy-two members to be examined.

To determine the effect that being accused of unethical behavior has on members' activity, two indicators of activity are used: roll-call voting participation rates and the number of remarks made on the floor.[10] Similar measures of activity have been used elsewhere (Frantzich, 1979; Herrick & Moore, 1993; Herrick et al., 1994; Hibbing, 1991). The voting participation rates and number of remarks made by the members during the Congress before an accusation was made were compared with the frequency of voting and remarks made during the Congress in which the accusation was made. The voting participation rates came from *Congressional Quarterly*'s *Roll-Call* from 1975 to 2000. These figures were simple percentages of the nonjournal roll-call votes cast by each member.[11] The number of speeches was calculated from the *Congressional Record*. All remarks listed as having been given by a member were included.[12]

The impact of accusations of ethical misconduct on legislative effectiveness or success was explored by measuring the accused members' ability to pass legislation they introduced while under the cloud of accusations. The measure that was used was similar to previous measures, in which either the percentage of bills passed or the number of bills passed is used as an indictor of members' ability to pass legislation (Frantzich, 1979; Herrick & Moore, 1993; Herrick et al., 1994; Hibbing, 1991). I decided to use number of bills instead of percentage of bills that a member introduced that passed because members may introduce bills without intending to see them pass. Thus, the number of bills is less biased by members' strategies on introducing bills. The expectation is that members will be less effective at passing their legislation after an accusation of unethical behavior is made than they were before the accusation.[13] To estimate members' ability to pass legislation, the number of bills they introduced that passed in the Congress of the accusation is compared to the number passed in the previous Congress.

Ideally, changes in the behavior of members accused in a given Congress would be compared to changes in the other members' behavior. However, a direct comparison is not really feasible because too few members were accused of unethical behaviors in a given Congress. Instead of directly comparing changes in the behavior of members accused of ethics violations with those not accused from Congress to Congress, I compare general Congressional trends in activity and effectiveness and general trends over members' careers with those changes in the behavior of members accused of violations. Research on legislative careers suggests that members become more active and more successful passing their legislation over the course of their careers (Frantzich, 1979; Hibbing, 1991). Also, the overall participation rates were increasing over the time period examined. In the 1970s participation rates tended to hover in the upper 80th percentile, and in the 104th Congress the average member attended over 95 percent of the votes (Mintz, 1996). Thus, most members would likely see an increase in their activity and effectiveness from Congress to Congress and any decline found in accused members' activities or effectiveness were likely to be caused by the accusation of unethical behavior, since it has not been the norm for members to become less effective or active over the course of their careers.

The data indicate that allegations of unethical behavior decreased members' voting rates. The average percentage of votes cast in the Congress prior to the accusation was 93.7 percent, falling to 90.5 percent in the Congress of the accusation. It is possible that this average is deceiving, since a few members experiencing a large decline could bias the mean downward. Therefore, the percentage of members who experienced a decline in their participation rates was also examined. About 66 percent of these members experienced a drop in their voting participation in the Congress of the accusation, only 29 percent experienced an increase, and 6 percent experienced no change.

While being accused of unethical behavior caused members to cast a smaller percentage of votes, it did not cause members to speak less often on the floor of the House. In the Congress before the accusation, the average member accused of unethical behavior spoke 125 times, while in the Congress of the accusation the average member spoke 130 times. Thus, there would appear to be a slight increase in the number of speeches members make after being accused of unethical behavior. Even if the number of members who decreased their frequency of remarks in the House is compared to those who increased their remarks, a slight increase was detected. A total of 55 percent increased the frequency of remarks and 45 percent decreased the frequency of remarks. Therefore, there is no clear effect of accusations of unethical behavior on the frequency of members' speeches.

The evidence also suggests that there was a modest decline in the effectiveness of members who had been accused of unethical behaviors. In the Congress preceding an accusation these members on average saw 2.1 of their bills passing in the House; in the Congress of the accusation the number falls to 1.7. Similarly, looking at the percentage of members who were more or less effective indicates a weak trend. About 25 percent were able to pass more bills and 35 percent passed fewer bills during the Congress in which they were accused of wrongdoing than in the proceeding Congress. The remaining members experienced no change, with a large majority of these members having passed no bills in either Congress. Again, the expectation for membership generally is an increase in effectiveness throughout their careers (Frantzich, 1979; Hibbing, 1991). Thus, being accused appears to decrease the ability of members to be effective legislators.

It is possible that part of the reason the findings were not stronger is that the Republicans gained control of the House in the 104th Congress. Since the members of the majority party are better situated to pass legislation than those in the minority party (Frantzich, 1979), changes between the 103rd and 104th Congresses may have been caused by changes in party rather than accusations of unethical behavior. Therefore, the Republicans accused of corruption in the 104th Congress may have been more likely to be effective in the 104th than in the 103rd Congress because of the Republican takeover. To correct for this possible problem, members who were accused in or after the 104th Congress were eliminated from the analysis. This left sixty members. Examining these members demonstrates a much sharper decline in effectiveness. In the Congress before the accusation, these members averaged passing 2.5 bills, falling to 1.7 in the Congress of the accusation.

In summary, the findings suggest that being accused of unethical behavior decreased members' ability to legislate. Although members accused of unethical behavior still speak on the floor, they miss more votes and see fewer of their bills passing in the chamber. That members who have been accused of unethical behavior were less able to work on legislation has important implications for the principle of fairness. Fairness involves members being able to fulfill their legislative obligations and accusations of unethical behavior limit members' ability to legislate. This harm to the fairness principle is particularly problematic when members are innocent of the accusations. These members and their constituents are denied an effective voice without cause and if the accusation was made in malice the unfairness of the situation becomes that much more apparent.

CONCLUSION

The goal of this chapter was to examine the degree to which ethics investigations harm Congress's and its members' ability to legislate. Generally, the findings suggest that investigating members' unethical behaviors had a modest effect on the ability of Congress to legislate. When Congress investigates its members it is still able to pass major bills. Some residual effects of the investigations were found with regard to Congress's ability to pass bills generally. In the quarter following news accounts of major investigations Congress saw fewer bills being passed. Since there was a lagged effect of investigations on bill passage, the effect seems more related to the environment that investigations caused than to the time spent on the investigations themselves.

The chapter also finds that being accused of unethical behavior had notable effects on members' ability to be active and effective legislators. Although these members still speak on the floor at similar levels prior to investigations, they cast fewer votes and see less of their legislation pass. Although these declines were fairly modest in scope, they do affect the fairness principle. Members who have been accused of unethical behavior become less able to fulfill their legislative obligations. This does not mean that ethics violations should not be investigated and disciplined. Rather, it indicates a need to insure that only valid allegations are investigated and that it is important to prevent violations in the first place. These are two issues that will be addressed further in the concluding chapter. In the next chapter, however, I develop and test a model to help explain which members are likely to be accused and convicted of violating the ethics standards. This is done to help identify ways to improve the ethics process, and to identify potential bias in the system.

NOTES

1. Although some of the data in Chapter 2 did find that following the 1977 reforms the number of violations went down when compared to the period just before it, both periods were part of the ethics climate that dates back to the 1960s.

2. Analysis was also conducted with year as the unit of analysis. Whether year or quarter was used did not alter the conclusions. Quarter was used since it increased the number of cases and degrees of freedom.

3. See Chapter 3, note 8 for more details on how Mayhew (1991) determined major legislation.

4. I analyzed the correlations between media coverage and number of resolutions debated to discipline a member, the number of votes on these resolutions, and the number of pages in the *Congressional Record* dealing with debate on these resolutions. The number of pages is used as an indicator of the amount of time spent on the debate. The correlations were high. The correlation between number of stories and votes was .56 (p. = .12); it was .31 (p. = .41) for resolutions and .59 (p = .09) for pages. The correlations do not meet normal levels of statistical significance because there were only nine cases. The correlations were calculated using a Congress as the unit of analysis.

5. I examined correlations between the variables to check for signs of multicollinearity. The only correlation over .5 was between overrides and vetoes ($r = .61$).

6. See Chapter 3, note 7 for a discussion of regression.

7. Since the data set includes the entire population and not a sample, the value of measures of statistical significance is debatable. I report the level of statistical significance for those who find them helpful.

8. This includes House resolutions introduced by the House Committee on Standards of Official Conduct that received debate on the floor. The resolutions are limited to those involving investigations; either the authorization of an investigation or approval of an action against a member.

9. I also examined whether being accused affected members' relationships with their party by looking at changes in party support scores. Members did not appear to alter their party voting in response to being accused of unethical behavior.

10. Bill introductions were not examined since most bills are introduced early in a term and more are introduced in the first than in the second term. Because of this, accusations of unethical behavior may come too late to affect bill introductions.

11. Remember too that House rules prohibit members accused of some crimes from voting.

12. This includes extension of remarks.

13. For this analysis, seventy-one of the seventy-two members were examined. Rep. Frank Thompson (D, NJ) was eliminated from the analysis since he was an outlier. While most members passed about two of their bills per term, he had twenty-eight the year of the accusation and thirteen the prior year.

CHAPTER 6

Explaining Unethical Behavior

Violating the ethics standards is harmful to the legislative process. As discussed earlier, ethics violations can harm the legislative principles (Thompson, 1995), deplete legislative resources, harm the public's opinion of Congress, limit the ability of those accused to fulfill their obligations, and make it more difficult for Congress to pass legislation. Since unethical behavior is harmful to the legislative process, in this chapter I examine what factors help predict whether a member is apt to violate the standards. In order to devise ways to improve the ethics of members it is necessary to determine what causes members to behave unethically. Some of the analysis in this chapter will also help detect bias in the system. By examining the types of members who were accused and the types who were convicted, it is possible to identify whether members with certain characteristics were less likely to be convicted than others. This chapter tests how well a simple model explains the likelihood a member will violate the ethics standards. The model suggests that members' opportunity to violate the standards plus their propensities to do so minus the costs explain whether members will engage in unethical behavior.

This model is based in large part on theories concerning Congressional careers. The literature on political ambition suggests that opportunity and costs of advancement affect members' career goals (Abramson, Aldrich, & Rohde, 1987; Brace, 1984; Frantzich, 1978, 1979; Hibbing, 1982; Kiewiet & Zeng, 1993; Rohde, 1979; Schlesinger, 1966). Members of the House who can run for an open Senate seat, for example, are likely to run for the Senate because they have a greater opportunity to win than those who face an incumbent. Similarly, members' post-Congressional careers are affected by the opportunities that are afforded former members (Herrick & Nixon, 1996). The costs of seeking office will also affect members' career decisions. House members who hold power positions are unlikely to run for the Senate, since they risk losing a powerful position by running for another office (Rohde, 1979). That is, members who gain significant seniority or leadership positions are less likely to run for the Senate than other members, all else being equal.

Although unethical behavior is not normally seen as a career path, the factors affecting the decision to violate the standards may fit similar categories as those affecting other career-related decisions. Members with the opportunity to violate ethics will be more likely to do so, and members differ in their opportunities. Members with leadership positions have more favors to offer for their own gain. Also, the length of members' service likely affects the opportunities members have to violate the ethics standards, since the longer they serve the greater the odds are that they have been tempted to violate the standards. Unethical behavior, like seeking a higher office, involves some risk, since members who are caught are likely to incur costs. Therefore, members who are likely to perceive greater costs if they are caught should be less likely to violate ethics than others. Although some costs should be a constant (two members who commit the same act, for example, should have the same punishment), some costs vary from member to member. Members who want to advance to a higher position may fear that violating ethics standards now will be a liability later. Thus, the perceived cost may be greater for members with progressive ambition than others. Another potential cost that could vary from member to member is electoral costs. Members who are electorally secure may be better able to withstand accusations of ethical misconduct than those who serve competitive districts (see Chapter 4).

Although the Congressional career literature has assumed similar levels of ambition or desire for members (Rohde, 1979; but see Herrick & Moore, 1993), the desire or propensity to violate ethics is not likely to be a constant. If members did not have a desire to serve they would not be in the House and all would take a higher office if offered to them. Their moral development, however, is not likely to be constant. Psychologists and others have noted that people differ in their moral development and in how they make decisions about ethical dilemmas (for example, see Kohlberg, 1984). Consequently, some members will use different criteria in making decisions and some will be more apt to violate the ethics standards. Variations in members' needs may also affect their propensity to violate the standards. Even if under normal circumstances a member is unlikely to behave unethically, members who feel backed against a wall may change their behavior. For example, members who need money to win their campaigns may be more likely to accept questionable contributions than members with large war chests or no challengers. In addition, members may vary in their propensity to violate the ethics standards because they differ in their carelessness or ignorance. That is, some members may be more likely to make mistakes that violate the standards. They fail to understand the rules or make errors in reporting their finances on financial disclosure forms.

Before proceeding to test the model, a description of the data is needed. This chapter examines members who served after 1976 and entered prior to 1994. Members entering after 1994 were not examined to give members ample time to violate the standards.[1] Accusations against these members that occurred prior to the 107th Congress are included in the analysis. Also, members who only served one term were eliminated from the analysis. Although these members may have had time to violate the standards, most will not have had time to be caught and investigated.

To determine which of these members behaved unethically, I rely on two measures. First, I examine all members who were accused of violating the House ethics rules or the law. Accusations are examined since the House often fails to punish members, even those who likely violated the rules. Thus, only examining members who were found guilty of violating the standards may miss numerous cases of actual violations. The method used to select these cases was discussed in Chapter 4. The cases are listed in Appendix A. Since few members were charged with more than one violation, this chapter examines only whether a member was charged instead of the number of times a member was charged. Of the 874 members in the population, 101 (12%) were charged with some type of violation.[2]

The second measure of whether or not a member behaved unethically limits cases to those in which the member was found guilty or convicted of a violation. This measure has a different set of biases than the previous measure. While the previous measure undoubtedly included members who were innocent of all charges, this measure likely ignores members who for one reason or another were never convicted of a violation even though a violation occurred. Using both measures helps insure that the findings are not biased in either direction. That is, conclusions that can be drawn by both measures are stronger than those that are just found with one. Also, noticing differences in the model's performance on the two measures may help identify biases in the process. If there are biases in the system then some types of members who are more likely to be accused would not be more likely to be convicted. To determine who was convicted I examined the members who were accused of violating the rules in the House or violating the law. Members who received an official punishment from the House, such as a reprimand, censure, or expulsion, were considered to have been found guilty. Second, members who were not punished but resigned after the House Committee of Standards of Official Conduct recommended a sanction or if the committee or House deemed a member's behavior a violation of a rule, even if no punishment was recommended, were considered to have behaved unethically. For example, Rep. Dick Armey (D, TX), who admitted to improperly using his letterhead, is considered to have behaved unethically even though the House committee recommended no punishment. In addition, members who were found guilty or pleaded guilty to some violation of the law are considered to have behaved unethically, whether or not the House took any action. Using this measure, sixty-eight of the members were considered to have behaved unethically. This figure indicates that about two-thirds of the time members who were accused of violating the ethics standards were convicted and that about 8 percent of the membership was convicted of some form of ethics violation.

One potential reason there were not more convictions was because of frivolous tit-for-tat charges. For example, while Speaker Gingrich was being investigated charges were levied against several Democratic leaders. While some of these accusations were legitimate, others were dismissed quickly by the ethics committee. But how many tit-for-tat allegations are made is impossible to say. It should also be noted that frivolous or false charges are likely to damage the legislative process itself. First, since accusations decrease public approval of Congress members, they harm the accountability principle. Second, since accusations divert attention from lawmaking, unfair accusations harm the fairness principle. Members defending themselves from accusations cannot fully carry out their duties.

Another potential reason there were not more convictions is because of the system of self-discipline. Although legal convictions are conducted through the courts, violations of House rules are investigated and tried in the House. As noted in Chapters 1 and 2, House members have a difficult time judging their colleagues. Members develop friendships and are dependent on each other to reach their goals. In addition, the process is often partisan.

OPPORTUNITY

One set of factors that should affect whether a member violates the ethics standards is opportunity. The Washington environment offers members many opportunities to take advantage of the system for personal or political gain. They could accept illegal campaign contributions, convert their office funds for personal use, and so on. However, some members may have greater opportunities than others. There are two means by which members may vary in their opportunities to violate ethics. One is power, or institutional strength, and the other is time in office. Members with greater power have more favors to grant in exchange for personal or political gain than do other members. Also, members who have served long tenures not only gain power but have more time to have behaved unethically.

One way members gain power is by garnering leadership positions. Members who hold party leadership positions or committee chairmanships have more power than other members. Favors from these members are actively pursued by political action committees (PACs), other members, interest groups, citizens, and businesses because they have a greater ability to deliver on promises than other members. Thus, these members are likely to have many opportunities to trade favor for favor, perhaps crossing the line set by the standards. At first blush it would seem as though leaders are more likely to violate the standards than others. With the exception of Dennis Hastert (R, IL), all speakers since and including Tip O'Neill (D, MA), and several floor leaders and whips (John Brademas [D, IN], David Bonior [D, MI], Richard Gephardt [D, MO], Dick Armey [R, TX], Tom Delay [R, TX], and Tony Coelho [D, CA]), have been accused of ethical misconduct at some point in their careers. Several of the violations have been severe. The charges against Speaker Wright were strong enough that he stepped down to avoid sanctions, and the charges against Speaker Gingrich led to a reprimand and fine. Even though the accusations against Reps. Tom Foley (D, WA) (bribery and misuse of office in 1977) and O'Neill (extortion in 1977) were never formalized, they were serious charges that may have had different results in later Congresses.[3] Several committee chairs have also been punished for ethics violations. Two committee chairs (Reps. Frank Thompson [D, NJ] and John Murphy [D, NY]) were involved in Abscam. Rep. Dan Rostenkoski (D, IL), long-time chair of Ways and Means, was sentenced to prison for embezzlement. Several subcommittee chairs have also lost their seats due to unethical behavior: Daniel Flood (D, PA), Harold Ford (D, TN), Robert Garcia (D, NY), Gerry Studds (D, MA), and Nicholas Mavroules (D, MA). To see whether leaders were more likely to be accused or convicted of violating the ethics standards, members who were either party leaders (speaker, floor leader, or whip) or standing committee chairs from 1977 to 2000 were identified. These members were coded 1 and the others 0.

A second source of power comes from being a member of the majority party. Members of the majority party also have power and thus opportunities for unethical behavior. Members of the majority party control the rules committee and hold committee chairs and many other power resources that can be used to increase their political power or personal wealth. Stewart's (1994) examination of the House banking scandal found that members in the majority were more likely to have bounced checks. Although Stewart did not find a relationship between bouncing checks and electoral security or being a committee chair, he did find Democratic members more likely to have bounced checks than Republicans. To test whether being in the majority party affects the likelihood that members violate ethics, using party label is not helpful since the House changed party control after 1994. To deal with this problem a three-point scale was used. Members who were always in the majority party were coded 2, those who were in the majority only part of their careers were coded 1, and those who were always in the minority party were coded 0.

Another factor likely to give members greater opportunities to violate the ethics standards is time. The longer members stay in office, the more likely they are to be caught up in the trappings of the office and come to expect special treatment. According to Rosenthal (1996), "Because of the intense nature of their work and the fact that they are constantly at risk, a sense of power and entitlement develops among members of a legislative body to which legislators become susceptible" (p. 32). Also, all else being equal, the longer members serve the greater the odds that someone will approach them about performing a favor. All else may not be equal, however, and seniority may also increase members' power and thus their opportunities. To test whether time in office affects the likelihood someone violates the norms, I used how long members served in years. Members who remained in office following the 106th Congress were coded according to how long they served prior to 2001, and those who had completed terms were coded based on how long they had served prior to leaving.

PROPENSITY

Not only might opportunity affect members' ability to violate ethics, but so too might their desire to have the goods or services violating the standards offer, or propensity. People differ in their ethical standards, and consequently, some members will be more apt to violate ethics. Some members, such as Rep. John Jenrette Jr. (D, SC), who was stung in Abscam, have "larceny in their blood" (this was said by Jenrette as quoted in *Congressional Ethics: History, Facts, and Controversy*, 1992, p. 65), while others are beyond reproach. Besides differing in their ethics standards, some members may have greater needs than others and these members may be more likely to violate the standards in order to meet those needs. For example, poorer members may have financial problems and trade money for favors out of desperation. Another way members may differ in their propensity is that some members are more likely to make mistakes that violate the rules than are other members. In the 99th Congress, for example, the ethics panel determined that both Reps. John Weaver and Dan Daniel had violated the rules but recommended no action since the mistakes were unintentional. Since direct measures of members' ethical values or carelessness are not available, I estimate propensity to violate ethics by relying on members' characteristics. Four possible characteristics are used to estimate members' propensity to violate ethical standards: gender, age, wealth, and partisanship.[4]

Members' gender may affect their propensity to violate ethical standards. Research on gender differences generally offer a couple of reasons to expect gender differences in ethical decision making. First, Americans often stereotype female politicians as more honest than male politicians (Leeper, 1991; Sapiro, 1981–1982). Thus, Americans expect there to be differences. Second, some feminist theorists argue that because of women's role in society, they have a different approach to issues of morality. One version of this view argues that because women's role in society is more nurturing than men's role, women's approach to moral problem solving is more likely to involve their effects on relationships (see Gilligan, 1982). Stereotypes and this feminist perspective suggest that female House members may be more likely to behave ethically than their male colleagues. The gender variable was coded 0 for men and 1 for women.

Age may also affect compliance with ethical standards. Young members may have less money but need more. As Rep. Ron Dellums (D, CA) said during debates on limiting members' outside income, "Some of the old codgers here that have put their children through college and paid off the mortgage, you do not care [about outside income]" (quoted in "Carter Signs," 1978, p. 847). Younger people are also less experienced and may be more likely to make mistakes. Stewart (1994) found that the younger members were when they entered the chamber, the more likely they were to have bounced checks at the House bank. Age was measured as members' age when they entered the institution.[5] Data for members' age comes from the *Almanac of American Politics* (Barone, Ujifusa, & Matthews, various years).

Members' wealth may also contribute to the likelihood that they will violate ethics. Members who are wealthy are less likely to need money, either personally or for campaigns. For example, a member worth millions of dollars is less likely to be attracted by a $10,000 bribe than a member with debts. Thus, either for their campaign or for their personal expenses, wealthy members are likely to have the money needed to pay their expenses. There is some support for the notion that wealth is related to compliance with ethics standards. Stewart (1994), for example, found that wealthier members were less likely to have kited checks than less wealthy members were. Also, it is likely that wealth does not affect members' ethics standards but that the rules are designed more to catch violations made by poorer members. Thompson (1995, p. 148) suggests that the types of ethics violations less wealthy members are convicted of are easier to spot and convict (e.g., bribery) than those committed by wealthy members (e.g., conflict of interest).

Members' financial disclosure forms are used to estimate members' wealth by subtracting members' reported holdings from their reported liabilities. Determining an individual member's holdings and liabilities is not as straightforward as it might seem. While members are required to disclose their financial holdings, earnings, debts, and transactions, they do not provide a specific dollar figure for each item but only provide a category for each holding, earning, and so on. For example, a member would list a specific liability and then specify that it was valued between $15,000 and $50,000. Following Stewart (1994), I used the middle dollar figure for each category to estimate the value of the item. Further complicating the estimation is that the largest dollar category does not have a middle and changed over the time of the study. In 1978 the largest category was over $100,000 (which has no middle), and therefore it was assumed that the item was worth $250,000. For the forms following 1978 the largest category was $250,000 or more. Here $400,000 is used as an estimate of the value of the liability or holding. For members entering in the 1990s the largest dollar category was greater than a million. For this category $2 million was the estimated worth. For members who entered prior to 1978, the 1978 disclosure forms were used. For members entering after 1978, their first financial disclosure form was used. Since the data collected cover a twenty-year period and American salaries and the cost of living have increased, members' net worth was standardized using 1992 dollars.[6] Given the problems with this measure, members were put into one of four categories. Members who were in the wealthiest quartile were coded 4, those in next wealthiest 3, the next to the lowest quartile were coded 2, and the poorest members coded 1.[7]

The partisanship of members may be related to their ethical behavior as well. The expectation is that highly partisan members will be more likely to violate the ethics standards than less partisan members. Members with strong party ties are likely to be acquainted with machine-style politics, which is notorious for unethical behavior (Benson, 1978). Also, partisan members may feel a greater allegiance to the party and politics than to ideals of ethics. To measure strength of partisanship, the average party unity score as reported in *Roll Call* (various years) for each member was examined.[8]

COSTS

Members' perceptions of the costs they may incur by violating the ethics standards may also affect their willingness to violate the standards. Members who believe they are risking little by violating the ethics standards should be more likely to violate ethics, while those who see greater risks should be less likely to violate them.[9] There are two indicators of potential costs: ambition and electoral survivability. First, members who have progressive ambition (desire for higher office) may see a greater risk in violating the standards than do other members. According to Schlesinger (1966), a key tenet of ambition theory is that members' ambition affects their behavior. Although this tenet has been supported by several studies (Francis & Kenny, 1996; Herrick & Moore, 1993; Soule, 1969), the effect of political ambition on unethical behavior has not been explored. It is widely speculated that members with strong ambition will do anything to increase their power, even if it means violating ethics. It is equally possible, however, that ambition limits members' willingness to violate ethics. Since there tends to be more information and better competition with elections for higher office, members with progressive ambition may fear that unethical behaviors—if caught—will limit their upward mobility. Most examinations of ambition have compared members with progressive ambition (the desire for higher office such as senator or governor) with those with static ambition (the desire to keep one's current position). Following this trend, I compared members who eventually ran for higher office (coded 1) with those who did not (coded 0). This measure of ambition may be biased, since members who want to run for a higher office but have violated ethics standards may choose not to run for higher office (although three members ran for higher office the election following an accusation of corruption). Nevertheless, it is used since it is the most common measure of progressive ambition.

Another way to measure ambition is by whether members have law degrees. Using whether a member has a law degree as a measure of ambition is not a measure of progressive ambition but of a general long-term desire to have a political career. Since a degree in law is often seen as a stepping-stone into politics, members who went to law school are assumed to have been planning a political career since they were in college. Although more members are elected today without a law degree than previously, for the time period of this study having a law degree was likely a sign that a member had thought about a political career since early adulthood. Consequently, they are likely to have a history of political ambition. There is some empirical support for these ideas. In an examination of the difference between lawyers and nonlawyers in the Ohio state legislature, Eakins (2002) states, "In summary, the data thus far seem to paint somewhat different portraits of lawyer and non-lawyer legislators with respect to their political ambition. Lawyers tend to be more likely to win office at an earlier age, indicate a long term interest in politics, indicate that they decided to run for the legislature on their own, and have aspirations for other office" (p. 9). To determine which members were lawyers, members' occupations and education listed in the *Almanac of American Politics* was used. Members who either have law degrees or list being a lawyer as their occupation were coded 1, others were coded 0.

Whether or not members believe they can survive an allegation of unethical behavior may also affect the likelihood that they will violate ethics standards. Here, survivability means electoral survivability. Members are concerned about keeping their seats and being reelected (Mayhew, 1974a); consequently, their electoral prospects may also affect whether they will violate the ethics standards. Members whose constituents would not tolerate unethical behavior are unlikely to take advantage of opportunities to violate ethics for fear of losing reelection. There are two ways that survivability may affect the likelihood of violating ethics. First, members who represent constituents who are intolerant of ethics violations will likely be constrained in their behaviors. Members who believe that their constituents will vote them out of office if they violate ethics should be less likely to violate the standards because they may lose reelections. Second, members who tend to win reelection by large margins may be willing to risk an allegation because they believe they can better withstand the allegation and still be returned to office.

One way members may gauge the likelihood that the voters will tolerate unethical behavior is constituents' levels of education.[10] Constituents who are well educated are likely to be more demanding of their members than are other constituents (Hibbing and Theiss-Morris, 1995, pp. 151–152; Verba, Schlozman, & Brady, 1995). Well-educated constituents are also likely to be aware of their members' behavior. Thus, well-educated constituents should be less likely to elect and reelect unethical members. To measure levels of education in a district, the percentage of constituents in the district with a college degree as reported in *Congressional Districts* (1973, 1983, 1993) was used. These data were calculated from the U.S. Census. For members in office during the 1970s, the 1970 data were used. For members entering after 1982, the 1980 data were used. For members entering after 1992, the 1990 data were used.[11]

In addition to constituent's levels of education, members' electoral security may affect their perceived costs of violating the standards, since it may affect their ability to survive an allegation of unethical behavior. If members' inability to withstand accusations of unethical behavior is a cost, then members who win reelection with small margins of victory will not violate the ethics standards. In essence, members who win with large margins can lose a small percentage of the vote and still win reelection, but those who barely win cannot. While this is the argument made here, it is possible that members who are electorally vulnerable will have a greater propensity to violate the standards as a means to win reelection. Members facing tough competition may be more likely to accept illegal moneys, use their staff to sway voters, or otherwise violate the rules in order to win. If this is the case, however, the direction of the relationship would change. Members coming from marginal districts would be more likely to violate the ethics standards than would members coming from safer states.[12] Thus, the data will indicate which argument is better supported empirically. Electoral security was measured by members' first reelection vote percentage. The first reelection vote was used, since all members in the data set ran for reelection at least once.

FINDINGS

Table 6.1 presents the variables' means. Eleven percent of the members have been leaders. On average they served about thirteen years, spending part of the time as a majority member and part as a minority member.[13] Average members were forty-three years old when they entered Congress, scored a 2.5 on the wealth scale, and voted with the party 81 percent of the time.[14] Seven percent of the members were female, 12 percent exhibited progressive ambition, and 43 percent were lawyers. The average member was reelected the first time with 68 percent of the vote and represented a district where 13 percent of the constituents had a college degree.

Table 6.1 also provided bivariate correlations between the independent variables and the dependent variables. One dependent variable measured whether members were accused of violating ethics and the other whether they were convicted of violating the ethics standards. The bivariate analyses support the model. All the measures of opportunity were statistically significantly related to being accused of unethical behavior in the expected direction. Members with leadership positions and in the majority party were more likely to be accused of violating ethics. Similarly, the longer members served, the more likely they were to have been accused of unethical behavior. The importance of opportunity was less significant when predicting which members were convicted of violating the standards. Of the three opportunity variables, only party was significantly related to being convicted of violating the standards although the direction of the relationship between conviction and leadership and seniority were in the predicted direction.

Table 6.1
Variable Means and Correlations with Accusations and Convictions

	Mean	r with accusation	r with conviction
Unethical Behavior	.12	—	—
Conviction	.08	—	—
Opportunity			
Leadership	.11	.14***	.04
Majority party	1.14	.11***	.11***
Seniority	13.20	.08**	.04
Propensity			
Party support	80.98	.09***	.07**
Wealth	2.5	−.14**	−.12***
Age	43.22	−.07**	−.04
Sex	.07	.03	.03
Costs			
Progressive ambition	.12	−.08**	−.08**
Lawyer	.43	−.06*	−.05
Constituent education	13.24	−.13***	−.10***
Reelection percentage	67.85	.05	.08**

*< .10; **< .05; ***< .01

Key: Unethical behavior: 1 = accused of unethical violation; 0 = not accused

Convicted: 1 = convicted of unethical violation; 0 = not convicted

Leadership: 1 = leadership position; 0 = no leadership position

Majority party: 2 = member always in majority; 1 = member sometimes in majority; 0 = member never in majority

Seniority: number of years served prior to 2001 or total number of years

Party support: average party support scores

Wealth: 4 = member in top quartile; 3 = member in second quartile; 2 = member in third quartile; 1 = member in bottom quartile

Age: age when entered the House

Sex: 0 = male; 1 = female

Progressive ambition: 1 = ran for higher office; 0 = did not run

Lawyer: 1 = lawyer; 0 = not a lawyer

Constituent education: percentage of constituents with a college degree

Reelection percentage: percentage of vote in first reelection bid

The bivariate analysis also indicates that propensity affected ethics violations. Poorer members and strong party supporters were significantly more likely to be accused of ethics violations and to be convicted of ethics violations. The younger members were when they entered the House, the more likely they were to be convicted or accused of violating the standards, but the relationship was only significant for accusations. Only gender was not significantly related to being either accused or convicted of unethical behavior. That gender was not significantly related to ethics violations may be caused by the small percentage of women who have served (8%). Women were less likely to violate ethics: 8 percent of the women were accused and 5 percent were convicted, compared to 12 percent and 8 percent for men, respectively.

The bivariate analysis also indicates that members' perceived costs may affect ethics violations. Members with progressive ambition and those with law degrees were significantly less likely to be accused of violating the ethics standards. Also, members coming from well-educated districts were significantly less likely to be accused of violating the standards. However, being electorally vulnerable did not significantly affect the likelihood that members were accused of violating ethics. Members who were electorally secure were more likely to be convicted of violating the standards. Also, members with progressive ambition and with well-educated constituents were significantly less likely to be found guilty of violating ethics standards. While being a lawyer did not have a significant effect on being found guilty of violating the standards, the results were in the predicted direction.

Although Table 6.1 presented bivariate correlations between the independent and dependent variables, multivariate analyses are needed to check for spurious relationships. Logistic regression was used, since the dependent variables were dichotomous. Logistic regression provides Maximum Likelihood Estimates, which in this case indicate the logged odds that a member with certain characteristics will be accused of or found guilty of unethical behavior. Since this figure is not easy to interpret, to help the reader understand the findings the probabilities that members with particular characteristics were accused or convicted of unethical behavior are offered in Table 6.2 and discussed in the text. To do this, the probability of being accused was calculated for the average member. This was done by multiplying the MLE by the mean (rounded to the nearest whole number) for each variable, then adding these figures to the constant.[15] This figure is the Z. It is plugged into the following equation to estimate the probability that the average member was accused or convicted:

$$\text{Prob(accused/convicted)} = \frac{1}{1 + e^{-z}}$$

This probability is used as a base and compared to the probabilities for members with a score different from the mean on one characteristic. These

Table 6.2
Probabilities of Members with Certain Characteristics Being Accused and Convicted of Unethical Behavior

	Accused	Convicted
Average member	.10	.11
Leader	.20	.10
Always majority party member	.15	.18
Always minority party member	.07	.06
Wealthy (top quarter)	.08	.08
Poor (bottom quarter)	.18	.19
Party Support = 91%	.13	.14
Party Support = 71%	.08	.08
Progressive ambition	.03	.02
Lawyer	.07	.07
0% of constituents college educated	.24	.21
25% of constituents college educated	.04	.06
Reelected with only 50% of vote	.10	.08

probabilities are calculated using the same formula. First, I will examine how well the model predicts who was accused of unethical behavior (Table 6.3). Then I will examine how the model predicts who was convicted of unethical behavior (Table 6.4). Correlations between the independent variables were examined to see if multicollinearity was likely to be a problem. However, the correlations between the independent variables never exceeded .50.[16]

Table 6.3 examines which members were most likely to be accused of violating the standards. Although the model only modestly improves our ability to predict who will be accused, the multivariate analysis generally supports the bivariate findings.[17] First, two of the three opportunity variables were significantly related to whether members were accused of violating the ethics standards. Leaders were significantly more likely to be accused of unethical behavior than nonleaders. Using the information in Table 6.2 it is evident that leadership made a significant difference in the probability that a member was accused of unethical behavior. While the model predicts that the average member had a .10 probability of being accused of unethical behavior, the probability was .20 for a leader. Also, being a member of the majority party affected whether members were accused of unethical behavior. While the probability of a member who was always in the majority party with the characteristics of the average member being accused was .15, it was .07 for a similar member in the minority. Although members with powerful positions may have greater opportunities and thus be more likely to violate the ethics standards, there was

Table 6.3
Logistic Regression Predicting Accusations of Unethical Behavior

	MLE	S.E.
Opportunity		
Leadership	.77	.36**
Majority party	.44	.16***
Seniority	−.01	.02
Propensity		
Party support	.03	.01***
Wealth	−.33	.11***
Age	−.02	.01
Sex	−.23	.51
Costs		
Progressive ambition	−1.15	.49**
Lawyer	−.40	.24*
Constituent education	−.08	.02***
Reelection Percentage	.004	.008
Constant	−2.29	1.16**
Frequency of dependent variable		
Accused	12	
Not accused	.88	
Proportion correct		
Total	.89	
Accused	.04	
Not accused	.996	
Proportion reduction in error	.01	
Model Chi-Square	71.19 (d.f. = 11)	
Probability (chi-square)	.00	
N = 875		

*< .10; **< .05; ***< .01

no evidence in the multivariate analysis that the longer members stayed in office the more likely they were to violate ethics.

Table 6.3 also provides evidence that members' propensity to violate ethics was related to being accused of unethical behavior. Members who were weak partisans and were wealthy were less likely to be accused of violating ethics standards than were other members. While an average member with a party support score of 81 percent (the mean) had a probability of .10 of being ac-

Table 6.4
Logistic Regression Predicting Convictions of Unethical Behavior

	MLE	S.E.
Opportunity		
Leadership	−.11	.45
Majority party	.58	.20**
Seniority	−.00	.02
Propensity		
Party support	.03	.01**
Wealth	−.33	.13**
Age	−.02	.02
Sex	−.51	.64
Costs		
Progressive ambition	−1.80	.74**
Lawyer	−.41	.28
Constituent education	−.06	.03**
Reelection percentage	.02	.01*
Constant	−3.85	1.37***
Frequency of dependent variable		
Convicted	.08	
Not convicted	.92	
Proportion correct		
Total	.92	
Convicted	1.47	
Not convicted	100.00	
Proportion reduction in error	.00	
Model Chi-Square	52.69 (d.f. = 11)	
Probability (chi-square)	.00	
N = 875		

*< .10; **< .05; ***< .01

cused, a member with a party support score of 91 percent had a probability of .13 and the probability was .08 for a member with a 71-percent party support score. In addition, members' wealth appeared to affect whether they were accused of violating the ethics standards. The probability that a member in the top quartile of wealth was accused of unethical behavior was .08, while it was .18 for a member in the bottom quartile. While party support and wealth were related to whether members were accused of violating ethics, age and gender were not.

Factors likely to affect members' perceptions of the costs of violating the standards also affected their behavior. Members who wanted to advance to a higher office were less likely to be accused of unethical behavior. Members with progressive ambition and lawyers were less likely to be accused of violating the ethics standards than were others. The probability that a member with progressive ambition violated the standards was .03, while it was .07 for a lawyer and .10 for a similar member with neither of those characteristics. Although progressive behavior is a common measure of progressive ambition, it poses a problem in determining the nature of the relationship. It may be that ethical members can run for higher office, not that ambition per se causes ethical behavior. However, that lawyers were also less likely to violate the ethics standards improves confidence in the findings that ambition constrains members' behavior.

Also, factors that might make a member vulnerable to electoral defeat prevented them from being accused of violating the ethics standards. Although reelection percentage did not significantly affect whether a member was accused of violating ethics, voters' educational levels did. The probability of being accused for a member representing a district where no constituent had a college degree was .24, while it was .04 for a similar member representing a district where 25 percent had a college degree.

Table 6.4 reestimates the model used in Table 6.3 using a different dependent variable: whether a member was convicted of violating the ethics standards. Generally, these findings were similar to but weaker than the earlier findings. Two of the opportunity variables had similar relationships with convictions as they did with accusations. Members in the majority were significantly more likely to have been convicted of behaving unethically than those in the minority, and seniority was not significantly related to whether members were convicted of violating the ethics standards. While the model estimated that a member who always served in the majority party had a .18 probability of being convicted, a member who was always in the minority party had a .06 probability.

Unlike the findings with regard to accusations, whether members had a leadership position did not significantly affect whether they were found guilty of violating the ethics standards. One interpretation of this is that leaders were more likely to be falsely accused. If this is true it would be consistent with the argument that accusations of unethical behavior are used for political purposes. One party could better distract and demoralize the other party by going after a leader in that party than a rank-and-file member. Also, a member wanting publicity would likely get more attention going after a leader than a rank-and-file member. For example, Newt Gingrich's notoriety went up when he was a junior member accusing Speaker Wright of unethical behavior. Another equally plausible explanation is that leaders were just as unethical but were better positioned to fight an allegation. Members may be reluctant to vote against their leaders, whom they might need later for a committee assignment, favorable rule, piece of pork, or other favor. Certainly, further research is needed to determine whether leaders were more likely to be falsely accused or better withstand valid allegations, or both. In either event, leaders were not treated fairly. They either were unfairly accused or were treated more favorably during the investigation process.

The relationship between whether members were convicted of violating the ethics standards and their assumed propensity to violate ethics was similar to the relationship between being accused of violating the standards and the propensity variables. As with Table 6.3, those with low levels of party support and those who were wealthy were less likely to have violated the ethics standards. A member with a party support score of 91 percent had a .14 probability of being convicted compared to .08 for a member with a 71-percent party support score. The probability that a member in the top wealthiest quartile was convicted of wrongdoing was .08, compared to .19 for a member in the bottom quartile. However, the relationship between wealth and conviction was weaker than the relationship between wealth and accusation. This may indicate a bias in the system: Members with wealth were better able to fight an allegation of unethical behavior. Also, similar to the earlier results, gender and age were not significant factors in predicting unethical behavior.

The variables measuring members' perceptions of the costs of violating ethics standards were related to whether members were convicted of violating the ethics standards. As with Table 6.3, members who had progressive ambition and who represented well-educated voters were significantly less likely to violate ethics. Members with progressive ambition had a .02 probability of being convicted of violating the standards, compared to .11 for a similar member without progressive ambition. Members representing a district where 25 percent of the constituents had college degrees had a .06 probability of being convicted, compared to .21 for a member representing no college graduates. Although the relationship between being a lawyer and being convicted of unethical behavior was not statistically significant, lawyers were less likely to be convicted. Unlike the relationship between electoral security and accusations, however, members who were electorally secure (won their first reelection by a large margin) were less likely to be convicted of violating ethics than those who won by smaller margins. While the average member had a .11 probability of being convicted, a member who won the previous election with just 50 percent of the vote had a .08 probability of being convicted.

CONCLUSION

This chapter examined a fairly simple model designed to explain unethical behavior. Members' opportunity plus their propensity to violate ethics minus the costs associated with being caught affect their behavior. By using two measures of unethical behavior, one involving accusations and the other convictions, the data supported the model. Although the model was supported by the evidence presented in this chapter, there are some caveats. First, these findings were stronger when an accusation of unethical behavior was the dependent variable than when having been convicted of unethical behavior was the dependent variable. The exception to this was that members who tend to win reelection by larger margins were significantly more likely to be found guilty of violating ethics than were other members, but were not significantly more likely to be accused. The weaker findings may be explained by the number of convictions being relatively small, or they may indicate biases in the ethics process in the House. Most notably, that leaders were more likely to be accused but not more likely to be convicted than rank-and-file members indicates that leaders were either more likely to be falsely accused or unfairly positioned to fight accusations. In either event this indicates a problem with fairness in the system.

One reason to explore explanations for variations in ethical behavior was to provide insights on how to prevent unethical members from being elected. The findings indicate that voters have a significant role in affecting the ethical behavior of members. Since personal characteristics and ambition affected members' ethics, by selecting the right member, voters can help insure a more ethical chamber. Also, since members representing well-educated districts were less likely to behave unethically than other members, examinations of the role education plays may help further the cause of ethics. The findings also suggest that members who were likely to incur costs if caught violating the ethics standards were less likely to violate ethics. Thus, reforms that increase the likelihood that members will be punished will decrease unethical behavior. Combined, this indicates that members arrive in Washington, DC with conditions that will either foster or inhibit unethical behavior. It is their personal characteristics or the district characteristics that affect whether a member is likely to be accused or convicted of unethical behavior. Thus, voters can affect the likelihood that members behave unethically by insuring that ethical members are sent to Congress and that they are held accountable.

The findings, however, do not offer much support for those who argue that limits on the number of years members can serve will improve members' ethics. Although term-limit advocates argue that less politically ambitious members are more ethical, the findings here suggest the opposite. Members with progressive ambition were less likely to violate the current standards than were other members. In addition, the findings offer no support for the idea that long service or electoral security increase members' likelihood of violating the current standards.

The findings here are in many ways preliminary and look at the larger picture of ethics. This means there are several questions unanswered, but three additional questions are paramount. First, while one of the strongest and most consistent relationships was between members' wealth and their ethics, it is unclear why wealth constrains unethical behavior. Wealthy members may appear less likely to violate ethics because they can finance their own campaigns, because they are less tempted by personal financial gain, or because they violate ethics rules that are hard to detect. More research is needed to sort this out. Second, greater clarification of the role of district-level education on members' behavior is needed. There are two processes that could cause such a relationship: well-educated voters send more ethical members to Congress, or educated voters constrain members' behavior. Again, more research is needed to clarify this finding. Third, no effort to distinguish between types of violations is made. It may be that members who violate the standards for personal gain differ from those who violate them for political gain, or those who violate the standards for sex may differ from those who violate them for money. Further analysis of this is needed to better design a system that minimizes the harm caused by unethical behaviors to the legislative process.

The analysis of this chapter was conducted to identify how to improve members' ethics and the ethics process. In the next chapter I summarize the findings of this book and use this information to make recommendations as to how to improve the current ethics process.

NOTES

1. Some members entering after 1994 have been accused of unethical behavior. However, I did not include them since their peers may need more time to either behave unethically or be caught.

2. This number is larger than the number listed in Chapter 5 since it does not exclude members who left in the Congress of the allegation.

3. Rep. Foley was not a party leader at the time; however, he chaired the Committee on Agriculture.

4. Theoretically there are a few reasons to suspect that race would affect the likelihood members violate ethics independent of socioeconomic status or district characteristic arguments. However, I examined this relationship and found that race did not have an independent effect. Thus, I do not report those results. Similarly, I examined religion but had little theoretical reason to expect members of one faith to be more ethical than those of another. I used two classifications, fundamentalist and Catholic, and neither was significantly related to ethical violations.

5. I cannot use age when unethical behavior occurred because all members did not violate ethical standards. Also, looking at the age when members left would not indicate if members were relatively young at any point during their careers.

6. To standardize the scores, the inflation calculator supplied by the Bureau of Labor Statistics on its Web page (http://bls.gov/cpi/home.htm) was used.

7. I also examined the effect of wealth without using the ordinal measure and found that the ordinal measure had the strongest relationship to ethics convictions and accusations. Members were on average very wealthy. The mean on the interval variable was over $800,000.

8. For members entering prior to 1990 the score was based on averages from the 95th to the 102nd Congresses, or the terms that a member served within that period combined, so that each member has one overall average score. For members entering after 1990, the scores were based on the 103rd Congress. This was done because the

data were collected at different times. Also, since party support scores do not vary greatly over members' careers (Hibbing, 1991), it was expected that little error was introduced by using a slightly different measure.

9. While it is possible that some members who violate ethics are risk seekers and violate the standards for the risk, I chose not to examine risk seeking since this is even more difficult to measure than propensity.

10. I also examined a state's political culture, as discussed by Elazar (1972), but it had no significant effects on whether a member was accused or convicted of unethical behavior. Given this and assorted problems with the idea of political culture, these findings are not reported.

11. Since the percentage of Americans with college degrees has risen over the years, efforts to standardize college education were made. However, since the conclusions were the same whether the unstandardized or standardized measure was used, and since the theory suggests that college education, not relative levels of education, is important, the unstandardized figures were reported.

12. It is also possible that the relationship is curvilinear, with members at both extremes being more likely to violate ethics. However, tests were conducted to see if a curvilinear relationship existed and the analysis suggests a linear pattern.

13. Since this variable is ordinal, the median is also reported here. It was 1.00.

14. Since the wealth variable is ordinal, the median is also reported here. It was 3.00.

15. The constant is the logged odds of being accused (or convicted) when all the other variables are 0.

16. The only relationship that neared .50 was between seniority and leadership ($r =$ .49), but even with the leadership variable removed from the analysis seniority still did not meet normal levels of statistical significance.

17. Part of the reason there was not more improvement in the ability to predict accusations is because there is not more variance in the dependent variable (also see Chapter 4, note 13).

CHAPTER 7

Conclusion and Recommendations

For its first 150 years Congress lacked clear ethics guidelines as well as an infrastructure to insure that members behaved in an ethical manner. Starting in the mid-twentieth century, however, an ethics climate developed as the media, the courts, and Congress each paid more attention to legislative ethics. As a result of the ethics climate, by the end of the 1970s the House as well as the Senate became serious about ethics, developing stronger guidelines and an infrastructure to investigate and punish violators. The previous chapters suggest that the ethics climate and subsequent reforms improved the overall behavior of the House membership at relatively modest costs. However, more can be done to further improve members' behavior and reduce the costs associated with violations and investigations. This chapter summarizes the previous chapters and ends with three broad recommendations to improve the process of enhancing ethical behavior.

SUMMARY

The ethics reforms are valuable to the degree that they have improved members' behavior and Congress's ability to function. Generally, the findings in Chapter 2 confirm that the reforms improved members' behavior and improved Congress's ability to fulfill its responsibilities. A survey of former members conducted for this project indicated that many questionable activities were less common after the reforms than before them. Members were less likely to receive gifts and travel from outside interests, pocket honoraria, misuse the franking privilege and staff, use campaign funds for personal expenses, engage in sexual misconduct, appear intoxicated on the floor, or continue to earn a living outside of Congress while in the House. In addition, campaign finance laws have limited the potential for members to receive large sums of money from large donors. These reforms undoubtedly increased the likelihood that members fulfill the obligations stemming from the legislative principles of independence, fairness, and accountability and also reduced the likelihood of misusing legislative resources. By limiting members' ability to supplement their incomes from interest groups, businesses, or individuals, either by working for them or by receiving gifts and honoraria, the reforms limited the potential for members to base decisions on these interests instead of the merits of policy. The prohibition against using staff and the franking privilege for campaigning helped improve the fairness of elections by limiting resources that can aid in elections that are only available to members. In addition, by reducing the amount of income members can earn and by limiting honoraria, members are expected to focus on their House work and not their outside jobs. By prohibiting the use of Congressional resources for personal or political gain, the reforms help insure that these resources are used for legislating.

While the reforms may not have increased accountability (i.e., increased the public's approval of Congress), the negative effects of the reforms and the ethics climate were less significant than is often assumed. Although the reforms were designed to address Americans' concerns over Congressional ethics in order to increase public confidence, they also made the unethical behaviors of members public knowledge. Thus, it is often argued they decreased the public's approval of Congress. However, though Chapter 3 demonstrates public accusations of unethical behavior had negative effects on the public's attitudes toward Congress, the effects were fairly modest. It takes several news stories for approval ratings to be noticeably lower, but sometimes the coverage is extensive. In addition, when a member is disciplined approval ratings go up. What is perhaps most significant, the public generally blames the membership not the institution for ethical problems. Since it is the membership and not the institution that is blamed, the legitimacy of Congress and the legislative process appear not to be too greatly harmed by allegations of wrongdoing.

Following the ethics climate and reforms, members' compliance with ethics standards may have improved by increasing the odds that unethical members leave the chamber. Members who violated the ethics standards were more likely to leave the chamber in a given term than were other members. The more severely members were punished, the more likely they were to leave the House. However, it was not necessarily members who violated the legislative principles or misused legislative resources who left. Instead what most greatly affected whether members accused of unethical behavior left was whether they had a leadership position or were electorally secure.

While the reforms caused noticeable benefits to the legislative process, one must be careful not to overstate the case. By addressing behaviors that were observable and had the potential to cause problems to the legislative principles, they punish some behaviors that caused no problems while allowing some that do. Although campaign finance reform has limited some potential for abuse, as long as members need campaign donors some elements of indebtedness to outside interests will remain. Also, as long as members are able to raise more money than challengers are, elections will not be fair. Members have other unfair advantages over their opponents. Members engage in constituency services and pork barreling, activities that are not available to non-members, which help them win reelection. The reforms themselves also create some unfairness. Members who are accused of violating the ethics standards are not able to focus on legislating while they are defending themselves. Thus, they are not fulfilling their legislative responsibility while defending themselves. In addition, there is evidence that either leaders are unfairly accused or are better able to ward off discipline when they have behaved unethically.

The reforms, along with the general larger concern for ethics, may have also allowed new problems to arise. Most notably, by the 1990s problems of growing incivility and conflicts of interest were observed. According to the survey of former members of the House reported in Chapter 2, members believe that members of the 1990s were more likely to behave "in a manner that did not reflect credibly on the House" than at any other time in the past forty years. Certainly the image most Americans have of recent Congresses is that civility in Congress is at a low point.[1] Incivility or behavior that does not reflect credibly on the House harms Congress's ability to fulfill its obligations. Incivility increases the image many Americans have that there is too much conflict in Congress, and conflict in Congress harms the public's support of Congress (Hibbing & Theiss-Morse, 1995). In addition, for members to get along and pass legislation there has to be a certain degree of decorum in the House, and incivility harms the team spirit.

Another ethics problem believed to have become more common is conflict of interest. Members surveyed for Chapter 2 indicated that conflicts of interest (i.e., members having a financial stake in legislative decisions) increased in the 1990s. Conflicts of interest come in many forms, but generally involve a member personally benefiting from a decision. Normally this is thought of as a financial benefit, but can involve other benefits, such as political benefits. Some of the current rules were designed to deal with conflicts of interest. Members are prohibited from using their office or legislative information for gain, are not to vote on legislation if they have direct interest in it, cannot contract with other federal agencies, and are prohibited from doing favors for family members, including hiring them.[2] In addition, the financial disclosure requirements, honoraria and gift limits, prohibitions of members serving on board membership, and limits on outside earnings were designed to deal with conflicts of interest. One type of potential conflict of interest that remains stems from members who develop a sense of indebtedness to campaign donors, although previous research offers mixed evidence of the existence of behavior consistent with such indebtedness. One way to help alleviate this problem, public financing of campaigns, will be discussed later.

Another type of conflict of interest involves members who have significant investment in an industry or personal ties to an industry or business, such as former employment, family, or friendship ties. The business ties of Vice President Dick Cheney illustrate the point. When Cheney was CEO of Halliburton its subsidiary won a government contract to work on the security of U.S. embassies. Questions were raised recently over whether, as vice president, Cheney could meet with members of Congress about budget increases to further improve embassy security (Crabtree, 2002). Similar questions have arisen over Cheney's ties to the oil and gas industry and his work on U.S. energy policy. While knowing whether policy makers' business ties bias their decisions is important, even if they do not, they give the appearance of a conflict, calling into question any decision that is made. One way the current reforms deal with this is by prohibiting members from voting on legislation that could directly benefit them. The ban, while understandable, is both too limiting and not tough enough. It is too limiting because often members' interests overlap with constituents' interests. A member who owns a dairy farm, for example, would not be allowed to vote on dairy subsidies. Yet if this member represents a large number of dairy farmers, he or she would be forbidden from voting on behalf of the district. The ban is not tough enough because members can affect the nature of the bill without casting a vote. In fact, the work members do introducing and amending bills, and their committee work, have a much greater effect on legislation than casting one vote.

One approach to better deal with conflicts of interest is to allow members with conflicts to participate but to limit their institutional role (Thompson, 1995, pp. 56–58). Members could participate in debates concerning an industry they have an interest in but could not take a leadership role in the area, such as chairing a committee overseeing that industry. But any such limit would need to allow the member to still have meaningful participation in debates. Often members with a direct interest in a policy area have considerable knowledge to offer. For example, Rep. Tom Coburn, (R, OK), a medical doctor, participated in debates likely to affect his private practice, a conflict of interest. Yet in doing so he offered experiences and knowledge about medical practices unfamiliar to most members (see Peaden & Herrick, 2001). Thompson's idea of limiting members' roles would allow members to still offer their expertise and represent constituents without unduly influencing the outcome.

Not only may ethics standards still allow behavior harmful to the legislative process, they have had some—although generally modest—negative side effects. It was estimated that investigations of ethics can decrease the amount of legislation that passed. Chapter 5 reported that ethics violations can cause a decline in the number of bills passed although they do not affect the passage of major bills. Members who have been accused of unethical behavior do not provide their constituents the same level of representation they did prior to the accusation. Most notably, they miss roll-call votes while being investigated, denying their constituents the most visible form of representation. They also were less able to get their legislation passed. The concern with ethics may also harm the legislative process by decreasing the willingness of people to serve.

The reforms increased the costs and decreased the benefits of service. To some members the financial disclosure forms have been a burden in time and money. To others the loss of outside earnings caused them financial strain. Members also feel less honor in their service because their ethics are constantly being challenged by the press and opponents. These strains may not only distract members from their work, but may also decrease their willingness to serve.

IMPROVING THE PROCESS

This section makes three recommendations to improve members' ethics and the process of investigating and disciplining unethical behavior in the House. First, the recruitment and selection of members needs to better insure that ethical citizens hold elective office. Second, an outside commission needs to be created to help minimize the costs of prosecuting and investigating potential ethics violations. Primarily, the system of self-discipline needs to be augmented with an outside commission to investigate charges of unethical behavior. The current system of members serving as prosecutor, judge, and jury leads to biases and unwillingness to assign guilt. Finally, individuals who make false and frivolous accusations against members should be held accountable. False accusations not only harm the member who has been accused, but may harm his or her constituents, increase conflict in the House, and divert legislative resources away from lawmaking toward ethics investigations.

Recruitment and Selection of Members

As with crime or disease, unethical behavior is best prevented in the first place. Not only does prevention forestall whatever harm might have resulted from unethical behavior, but the fewer the investigations, the fewer resources are expended on ethics investigations. Also, there will be fewer constituents losing effective representation, and fewer dips in public approval. Thus, prevention of unethical behavior is invaluable. Clearly, one way to limit unethical behavior is to better insure that ethical people are selected in the first place. In fact, Chapter 6 demonstrated that members' propensity to violate ethics has the greatest influence on members' ethics. Since members vary in their predisposition to violate ethics, ethical people need to be recruited and elected to office. More than one of the former members I surveyed made a comment such as, "You can't legislate morality."

In the United States, political recruitment or candidate emergence is described as "self-starting": Candidates decide for themselves whether to run. Nevertheless, political parties do work on recruiting and could do more to encourage ethical people to run for office. As party officials and others encourage would-be candidates to seek office, they should be concerned with candidates' ethics as well as their electability. Some party officials are already concerned with ethics, if for no other reason than to avoid scandals that harm the party. Clearly, in nations and states where parties are active in the recruitment and nomination of candidates, the party and its officials should take into consideration a candidate's past as it relates to ethics. They should encourage candidates who have clean records and discourage those who have pasts indicating they may be inclined to violate ethical standards. Candidates who have faced legitimate ethical problems in the past should be discouraged from seeking office.

Parties cannot prevent candidates from seeking office, and some local party organizations may be disinterested in ethics; therefore, a number of unethical candidates will still appear on the ballot. Thus, voters also need to concern themselves with candidates' ethics. Chapter 6 suggests that voters play a key role in insuring that members behave ethically. As one of the former members surveyed said, "The electorate get the representation they deserve—a concerned, informed electorate will send and keep good ethical representation."

Increasing voters' interest in candidates' ethics is not easy. Society generally seems willing to accept unethical behavior or cutting corners to get ahead. Cheating is rampant on college campuses, esteemed writers such as Doris Kerns Goodwin and Steven Ambrose have been accused of plagiarism, countless CEOs have had legal problems for unethical business practices, and even little league baseball has not been spared allegations of cheating. Many voters have willingly elected representatives known to violate normal ethical standards. Rep. Alcee L. Hastings (D, FL) was elected to the House after being impeached and removed from the federal courts. Rep. James Traficant (D, OH) became a "folk hero" in his district prior to becoming a congressman when he successfully defended himself against racketeering charges (Singer, 2002). Yet evidence in this book suggests voters can play a significant role in insuring a more ethical House. Members representing well-educated constituents are less apt to have members who violate the ethics standards, and constituents living in competitive districts can remove unethical members at the ballot box.

One way to help increase voters' awareness of candidates' ethics and to give voters increased opportunities to vote for ethical candidates is to have more competitive elections. Competitive elections may help in two ways. First, they will increase the number of members facing accusations of unethical behavior who lose reelection or retire. Chapter 4 demonstrated that the greater members' electoral security, the more likely they were to return to the House following an accusation of unethical behavior. Members who face accusations of unethical behavior usually lose votes, but a member who starts off with 70 percent of the voters' support could lose 20 percent of their support and still win reelection. Thus, the more competitive the district, the greater is the likelihood that members facing allegations of unethical behavior will lose reelection. Members facing accusations who represent competitive districts may also be more likely to retire. Members who face tough reelection bids are more likely to retire than others, not wanting to invest their time, money, and energy only to be rejected by the voters. Second, competitive elections may even prevent the election of unethical members in the first place. Competitive elections should improve the ethics of members elected, since they are associated with higher-quality challengers. If challengers are poor-quality candidates, voters have little choice but to vote for incumbents, even if their behavior is questionable. Rundquist, Strom, and Peters's (1977) research suggests that voters will vote for unethical members if the candidate is preferable overall. Although a candidate's ethics may affect voters' preferences, so do party, leadership skills, issue positions, and so on. Thus, if districts are competitive and voters have real choices, they are likely to choose the ethical candidate. Since many districts favor one party over the other, the competitiveness of elections should include primaries. Quality challengers of the incumbent's party need to be willing to run against their partisans, especially if the incumbent has committed severe wrongdoing.

Competition can be increased in several ways. One way is to encourage more quality candidates to run for Congress. This could be done by creating districts where both parties are competitive. More party competition could occur through party-building activities or through the redistricting process. Improving the image of Congress could also encourage more people to run for Congress. Potential candidates would be more likely to throw their hats in the ring if public service was valued more in society. Term limits at the state level may increase competition for Congress. Carey, Niemi, and Powell (2000) found that in states with term limits state legislators were more likely to express a willingness to run for U.S. Congress than those in nonterm-limit states were. Essentially, as state legislators are forced out of office, those wanting a political career may seek a seat in the House. Before advocating for state term limits to increase competition, greater examination of the effects of term limits on the legislative process, including members' ethics, is needed. Term limits may increase conflicts of interest (Thompson, 1995) or have other negative effects on the legislative process.

Another way to increase competition and the willingness of quality candidates to run for the House is Congressional campaign funding reform. Incumbents can scare off decent challengers by having a stockpile of campaign dollars. If incumbents are able to scare off quality challengers, then elections are not fair and voters may not have the opportunity to elect the best representative. Although unpopular with Americans, federally funded campaigns may be the best way to increase competition and encourage more ethical people to run for office. Federally funded campaigns would even the playing field, at least in terms of money.[3] Removing the need to raise campaign funds may also improve members' ethics, since there is the potential that fund-raising makes members indebted to certain interests. If members become indebted, they are less likely to represent the district or make decisions based on the merits of the policies, violating the independence principle, although the research on the influence of PAC contributions on members' roll-call votes finds little support for a significant relationship. Campaign finance reform may also increase the odds that ethical people will want to run for and hold office. Although an investigation is beyond the scope of this book, it is likely that the need for campaign funding deters a number of would-be statesmen and women from seeking office. Thus, federally funded elections, in particular, could increase the ethics of members by encouraging ethical Americans to seek office and eliminate the potential that members' legislative behavior is affected by campaign donations.

Besides increasing competition, another way to increase the likelihood that voters consider candidates' ethics when voting is to increase information on candidates' ethics. The amount of information voters have about the candidates' ethics is likely to affect their selection. Competitive elections may improve voters' knowledge of members' ethics, since voters have more information in competitive elections due to heightened debate and media exposure. Another way to increase the information voters have about potential ethical problems is to make more accessible candidates' financial disclosure forms. Currently, candidates are required to disclose their liabilities and assets either by May 31 or within thirty days of the election depending on filing dates and campaign funds raised. However, this information is not discussed at the same level as the campaign funding information and is not easily obtainable for the average American. Greater attention to this information will help voters know the conflicts of interests each candidate is likely to have. Since conflicts of interest are endemic to representational democracy, it might be best to allow voters to decide what conflicts are acceptable instead of trying to legislate it.

Outside Commission

The second recommendation is the creation of a bipartisan, outside ethics commission to replace the Committee on Standards of Official Conduct. The idea of an outside commission has been advocated elsewhere. At testimony before the House Ethics Reform Task Force, Norman Ornstein (Brookings Institute), David Mason (Heritage Foundation), and Gary Ruskin (Congressional Accountability Project) spoke in favor of allowing more investigations by outsiders (U.S. House, 1997). Thompson (1995) advocates for an outside commission in his book on Congressional ethics. Also, at least one of the members interviewed for this project expressed support for an outside commission, "House committee on ethics 'Official Standards' does not serve well as accuser—investigator prosecutor and Judge—Should have former members as judges and only preliminarily activities by current members."

Although the commission could take many different forms, the primary responsibility of the commission would be to investigate accusations of wrongdoing filed by members and to recommend discipline if needed. Since the House has the Constitutional responsibility to discipline members, it would have to decide whether to follow the recommendation of the commission.

Certainly, giving the House the final say allows for self-judgment to remain. However, with an outside panel of experts indicating discipline is needed, it would likely make it hard for the House to ignore the report. To be successful the commission would need to be bipartisan; made up of an even number of Democrats and Republicans. Commissioners need to be individuals with a history of fairness and a bipartisan spirit. They would also need to be individuals with an understanding of the legislative process. Former members, former staffers, or academics would all be appropriate for membership.

The main value of an outside commission is that it would supplement the system of self-judgment, which is known for partisanship and a reluctance to discipline members. As pointed out in Chapter 2, because the current system involves members sitting in judgment of each other the ethics committee has a history of not wanting to discipline members and of partisanship. The commission could decrease partisanship, since commissioners would not be members of the House attending party conferences with an allegiance to their party in the House. An outside commission would involve a fresh start, with individuals not indebted to those being investigated. It would also reduce the need for members to sit in judgment of their colleagues and in turn improve the odds that members deserving discipline would receive it. Disciplining members is important. Congress can regain some prestige that it loses when members violate ethics standards when it opts to discipline the members. Chapter 3 found that public opinion rose when members were disciplined. Discipline can also increase the odds that members who violate the standards leave the House. Chapter 4 found that the stronger members' punishments, the more likely they were not to return to office. Therefore, a system of discipline that disciplines members appropriately will help insure that only ethical members serve in Congress.

The outside commission could also help insure that leaders are dealt with fairly. Chapter 6 indicated that leaders are unfairly treated in the current ethics process. Leaders are either more likely to face untrue allegations or are better able to defend themselves against accurate charges of unethical behavior. Bringing charges against members who file false charges could help in the first case and will be discussed later. In the second case, an outside commission could help insure that leaders who have violated the rules are treated the same as other members. Leaders in the House can either help or hurt the ability of rank-and-file members to accomplish their goals. Party leaders can influence such things as committee assignments, office space, and rules for debate on legislation, while committee chairs may affect favorable legislation coming out of their committees. Consequently, rank-and-file members may be reluctant to vote against leaders, particularly in their party. An outside commission made up of nonmembers would not be dependent on leaders for future favors, nor have the same concerns about passing judgment on leaders.

Another key advantage of an outside commission is that it would reduce the legislative time costs associated with investigating ethics. Members on the ethics committee spend about forty hours a term attending meetings and count-less hours investigating ethics outside of formal meetings.[4] These are hours the members could have spent making laws and representing constituents. The committee is often seen as one of the least desirable committees to serve on, as it does not help members reach their goals of affecting policy, being reelected, or gaining power (Fenno, 1973). Replacing the Committee on Standards of Official Conduct with an outside commission would also have the advantage of reducing scheduling conflicts, a perpetual problem in Congress, by decreasing the number of committees.

Proposals to create an outside commission have circulated in Congress over the past few years but are unpopular on Capitol Hill. It is feared that outsiders would not understand the legislative process and why some behaviors are needed. The 1997 House Ethics Reform Task Force rejected the idea. Task Force members were concerned with the explicit Constitutional responsibility of the House to discipline its members for wrongdoing. They expressed the view that House members better understand the rules, customs, and practices of the House, and they expressed the strong preference that House members accused of misconduct be judged by their peers (U.S. House, 1997).[5] Although the fears expressed by the task force are legitimate, they are not insurmountable. First, insiders such as former members and staffers, who understand the rules and norms of the House but are not part of the current House, could be put on the commission. The fear that Congress would be abdicating its duties instead of performing them could also be addressed if the commission's role was to investigate and recommend actions, leaving actual decisions on discipline to the House.

False Accusations

The final recommendation is to discipline members who make frivolous and false accusations. The political use of ethics violates the fairness and accountability principles and depletes legislative resources. Thus, to eliminate some of the negative effects of the ethics reforms, individuals who make false accusations should be held accountable. Disciplining individuals who file false complaints would take very little policy change. Currently, the only people who can file complaints to the House ethics committee are members, and the House clearly has the power to discipline its membership. Also, the code of conduct prohibits behavior that does not reflect credibly on the House: Making false complaints against a colleague does not reflect credibly on the House.

Holding members accountable for making false accusations, however, needs to be balanced with the need to allow members to make accusations. If members fear that by making what they believe is a legitimate charge they risk having their own ethics problems, many violations may go undetected. Therefore, the punishment should only be available to accusations that are clearly false. One way to create a balance is to only allow members of the ethics committee, or outside commission if created, to file complaints against members who file false accusations. This limits the number of members who can file such complaints, and denies those who have been accused from filing countercomplaints. It also allows those with the most information on the case to file the complaint. This would work best if an outside commission was created. The ethics panel has had a history of partisanship: Thus there is greater potential for abuse with this committee.[6] Another way to create a balance is to minimize punishments. Allowing punishments that are stronger than a public condemnation, such as expulsion or instituting large fines, are likely too severe and could inhibit the filing of legitimate complaints.

The twentieth century saw great improvements to the ethics process in the House of Representatives. Although at times the concern for members' ethics was abusive and excessive, members today are more ethical than at earlier times. Concerns about Congressional ethics are likely to remain well into the twenty-first century. These concerns are justified. Unethical behavior can clearly hurt the ability of Congress to legislate and represent constituents. However, investigations of unethical behavior and strong ethics standards can be costly to the legislative and representational functions of Congress as well. A reasonable balance between the costs and benefits of insuring ethical behavior could be achieved with greater care in selecting members, punishing members who make frivolous accusations, and establishing an outside commission to investigate charges of unethical behavior.

NOTES

1. Whether incivility is on the rise is in need of further investigation. Jamieson and Falk (2000), using the taking down of words process in the House to indicate lack of civility in the House, found no clear rise in incivility in House debates.

2. This is a summary of the House's highlights of the ethics rules (see http://www.house.gov/ethics/highlights2002.htm).

3. Even if all candidates had the same amount of money, incumbents would still have advantages. They would still have greater name recognition, the frank, constituency services, and pork barreling.

4. This figure was calculated by examining committee reports.

5. Since the task force realized there was a problem with committee members being overworked, they made a recommendation that was adopted. Now there is a pool of extra members who help the committee with its work. While this might help alleviate some of the work by committee members, it also will take even more members from legislating and representing to investigating ethics.

6. The 1997 Ethics Reform Task Force noted concerns with the partisanship of the process and made recommendations, which were adopted, to minimize partisanship on the committee. The reforms involved giving the minority party more influence over the agenda and insuring bipartisan staff. These reforms may be helpful, but as long as individuals who have direct benefits of being partisan are making the decisions, any reforms are likely to be ineffective.

Members Accused of Unethical Behavior

Representative	Charge	Outcome[1]
95th Congress		
Brademas, John	Koreagate	No punishment[2]
Burke, Herbert	Disorderly conduct	Conviction[3]
Diggs, Charles	Diverted funds	Censure/conviction
Eilberg, Joshua	Illegal compensation	Conviction
Flood, Daniel	Bribery/conspiracy	Conviction
Flowers, Walter	Koreagate	No punishment
Foley, Tom	Koreagate	No punishment
McFall, John	Koreagate	Reprimand
O'Neill, Thomas	Koreagate	No punishment
Passman, Otto	Koreagate	No punishment
Patten, Edward	Koreagate	No punishment
Richmond, Frederick	Solicited sex	Treatment[4]
Roybal, Ed	Koreagate	Reprimand
Wilson, Charles H.	Koreagate	Reprimand
96th Congress		
Bauman, Robert	Sex solicitation	Treatment
Carney, William	Illegal gratuity	Conviction
Hinson, Jon	Obscene act	Conviction
Jenrette, John	Abscam	Conviction

Representative	Charge	Outcome[1]
96th Congress (*continued*)		
Kelly, Rich	Abscam	Conviction
Leach, Buddy	Campaign finance	No punishment
Lederer, Ray	Abscam	Conviction
Murphy, John	Abscam	Conviction
Myers, Michael	Disorderly conduct and Abscam	Expulsion/conviction
Thompson, Frank	Abscam	Conviction
Wilson, Charles H.	Financial misconduct	Censure
97th Congress		
Murtha, John	Abscam	No punishment
Richmond, Fred	Tax evasion/improper influence/drugs	Conviction
98th Congress		
Burton, John	Drug use	No punishment
Crane, Daniel	Sexual misconduct	Censure
Dellums, Ron	Drug use	No punishment
Ferraro, Geraldine	Financial Disclosure	No punishment
Goldwater, Barry	Drug use	No punishment
Hansen, George	Financial Disclosure	Reprimand/conviction
Studds, Gerry	Sexual misconduct	Censure
Wilson, Charles	Drug use	No punishment
99th Congress		
Andrews, Michael	Misuse of office	No punishment[5]
Boner, William	Personal gain	No punishment
Daniel, Dan	Free rides	No punishment
Feighan, Edward	Misuse of office	No punishment[6]
Fiedler, Bobbi	Political corruption	No punishment
St. Germain, Fern	Personal gain	No punishment
Weaver, John	Personal gain	No punishment
100th Congress		
Biaggi, Mario	Illegal gift/disclosure	Conviction
Coelho, Tony	Misuse of office	No punishment
Ford, Harold	Influence peddling, bank, mail, and tax fraud	Conviction

Representative	Charge	Outcome[1]
100th Congress (*continued*)		
Garcia, Robert	Bribery/extortion	Conviction
Murphy, Austin	Vote fraud/misuse of office	Reprimand
Oakar, Mary Rose	Improper employment	No punishment
Rose, Charles	Misuse campaign funds/disclosure	No punishment
Stallings, Richard	Misuse campaign funds	No punishment
Sweeney, Mac	Misuse of office for campaign	No punishment[7]
Swindall, Patrick	Improper intervene/perjury/ money laundering	No punishment
Wright, James	Improper influence, illegitimate outside income/gifts	No punishment
101st Congress		
Bates, Jim	Sexual misconduct/misused office	No punishment
Dickinson, Bill	Illegal loan	No punishment
Dyson, Roy	Misused office	No punishment
Flake, Floyd	Fraud and tax evasion	No punishment
Frank, Barney	Misused office	Reprimand
Gingrich, Newt	Illegitimate income	No punishment
Lukens, Don	Sexual misconduct	Conviction
Savage, Gus	Sexual misconduct	No punishment
Sikorski, Gerry	Misused employees	No punishment
Stangland, Arlan	Illegal credit card charges	No punishment
102nd Congress		
Alexander, Bill	Conflict of interest	No punishment
Alexander, Bill	House bank	Cited[8]
Bustamente, Albert	Racketeering	Conviction
Clay, William	House bank	Cited
Coleman, Ron	House bank	Cited
Conyers, John	House bank	Cited
Davis, Robert	House bank	Cited
Early, Joseph	House bank	Cited
Edwards, Mickey	House bank	Cited
Feighan, Edward	House bank	Cited
Ford, Harold	House bank	Cited
Goodling, Bill	House bank	Cited

Representative	Charge	Outcome[1]
102nd Congress (*continued*)		
Hatcher, Charles	House bank	Cited
Hayes, Charles	House bank	Cited
Kolter, Joe	Post office	Conviction
Mavroules, Nicholas	Bribery, tax fraud, illegal gifts	Conviction
McDade, Joseph	Extortion, illegal gratuity	Conviction
Mrazek, Robert	House bank	Cited
Murphy, Austin	Post office	No punishment
Oaker, Mary Rose	House bank	Cited
Perkins, Carl	House bank	Cited
Rostenkoski, Dan	Embezzlement	Conviction
Solarz, Stephen	House bank	Cited
Towns, Edolphus	House bank	Cited
103rd Congress		
Ford, Harold	Conspiracy and bank and mail fraud	No punishment
Frost, Martin	Illegal redistricting	No punishment
Hubbard, Carroll	Misused employees	Conviction
Gingrich, Newt	Improper solicitation of funds	Reprimanded
Mavroules, Nicholas	Influence peddling	Conviction
Oakar, Mary Rose	Lying to FBI	Conviction
Reynolds, Bobby	Sexual assault	Conviction
Rose, Charles	Financial disclosure	Conviction
Smith, Larry	Tax evasion	Conviction
Tucker, Walter	Bribery	Conviction
104th Congress		
Armey, Richard	Letter on stationery	No punishment
Bliley, Thomas	Conflict of interest	No punishment
Bonior, David	Book deal, trips	No punishment
Collins, Barb	Misuse office, campaign	No punishment
Cooley, Wes	Embellished military record	Conviction
Gephardt, Richard	Real estate transaction	No punishment
Greene-Waldholtz, Enid	Campaign funding	No punishment
Kim, Jay	Campaign funding	Conviction
Kleczka, Gerald	Drunk driving	Conviction

Representative	Charge	Outcome[1]
104th Congress (*continued*)		
McDermott, Jim	Conflict of interest	No punishment[9]
McIntosh, David	Letterhead misuse	No punishment
Shuster, Bud	Illegal gratuity	No punishment
Soloman, Gerald	Threatened state officer to take action	No punishment
Wilson, Charles	FEC violations	Conviction
105th Congress		
Brown, Corrine	Illegal gifts	No punishment
Delay, Tom	Influence peddling	No punishment
106th Congress		
Hilliard, Earl	Diverted campaign funds for personal use	No punishment
Delay, Tom	Used office to threaten	No punishment

NOTES

1. The outcome may not have occurred in the Congress in which the accusation was made. Only members who were still in office when the accusation was made are included.

2. No punishment means that the member was not punished by the full House or a court of law. However, a member may have been found guilty of wrongdoing by the Committee on the Standards of Official Conduct.

3. Conviction refers to court proceedings. It may include pleading guilty or no contest. It may also include conviction or plea of a lighter office.

4. The member agreed to enter a treatment facility to have the charges dropped.

5. This case did not appear in the *Congressional Almanac* but did appear in Thompson (1995).

6. This case did not appear in the *Congressional Almanac* but did appear in Thompson (1995).

7. This case did not appear in the *Congressional Almanac* but did appear in *Congressional Ethics: History, Facts, and Controversy* (1992).

8. Many members bounced checks at the House bank. Only those who were "cited" by the House as abusing the House bank are listed.

9. This case was still in civil court when this book went to press.

Questionnaire Sent to Former Members

Please take a few minutes to answer the following questions:

1. How would you characterize the effects that ethical reform had on the chamber's ability to make policy that is in the public's best interests?

2. Did your behavior change in order to comply with the ethics standards? For example, did you stop taking honoraria, sell stock, limit your outside earnings, etc.

   ___ Yes   ___ No

   2b. If you changed your behavior, please explain.

3. Are you aware of other members who changed their behavior in order to comply with the ethics standards?

   ___ Yes   ___ No

   3b. If yes, please explain.

4. Please describe any costs, personal, financial, or in time spent, that you or other members incurred in order to comply with the ethics standards.

5. Do you believe the ethics standards address the worst behaviors? If not, what else should be covered?

6. I am interested in how common certain activities were at given points in time. Please indicate how common you believed it was for members of the House to engage in each of the following activities during the time listed, using a 10 point scale with 10 being very common and 1 not common at all. If you were not in the House during a given period please record a zero.

	1965–1970	1971–1976	1977–1983	1984–1990	1991–1996
Received honoraria	____	____	____	____	____
Received large gifts from lobbyists	____	____	____	____	____
Converted campaign or office funds into personal use	____	____	____	____	____
Used the frank for campaigning	____	____	____	____	____
Reimbursed for travel by lobbyists/ interest groups	____	____	____	____	____
Earned large outside income	____	____	____	____	____
Had a financial interest in a business affected by Congressional actions	____	____	____	____	____
Behaved in manner that did not reflect credibly on the House	____	____	____	____	____
Had staffers do non-official work	____	____	____	____	____
Appeared intoxicated on the floor of the House	____	____	____	____	____
Sexual misconduct	____	____	____	____	____

7. What is your political party?   ___ Democrat___ Republican

   Is there anything else you would like to tell me about ethical reforms and investigations?

Glossary of Key Scandals

ABSCAM. Abscam was the result of an FBI sting operation. FBI agents posed as Arab sheiks and offered bribes to members in return for favors. The transactions were recorded on videotape. Members were seen accepting large sums of money ($50,000 or so) in return for introducing private bills. On video, one member complained that the money was not enough while another bragged of having "larceny in his blood" (quoted in "'Abscam' Scandal," 1980, p. 516). Abscam resulted in one member, Rep. Michael "Ozzie" Myers (D, PA) being expelled, one member, Rep. John Jenrette (D, SC), resigning on the eve of expulsion, and four other members either losing reelection or eventually resigning before the House voted on sanctions. The members were also convicted in Federal Court of bribery, racketeering, accepting an unlawful gratuity, and conspiracy. Another member, Rep. John Murtha (D, PA), avoided charges by testifying for the government. Two of the members charged were committee chairs: Rep. John Murphy (D, NY) was chair of the House Merchant Marine and Fisheries Committee and Rep. Frank Thompson (D, NJ) chaired the House Administration Committee. Several members expressed concern that the sting operation involved entrapment and found it difficult to support sanctions ("'Abscam' Scandal," 1980, pp. 513–521).

REP. OAKES AMES (R, MA). See Credit Mobilier.

REP. MARIO BIAGGI (D, NY). In 1987, Rep. Mario Biaggi (D, NY) was convicted of illegal gratuity and obstruction of justice relating to a vacation he accepted after helping a ship builder. In 1988 he was convicted of bribery, racketeering, and extortion in relation to the Webtech case and resigned before the House voted to expel him. Webtech was a business that received numerous government contracts without submitting bids (*Congressional Ethics: History, Facts, and Controversy*, 1992, p. 69).

REP. JOHN BRADEMAS (D, IN). See Koreagate.

REP. JAMES BROOKS (D, NY). See Credit Mobilier.

REP. DANIEL CRANE (R, IL). See page sex and drug scandal.

SENATOR ALAN CRANSTON (D, CA). See Keating Five.

CREDIT MOBILIER. In 1873, Reps. Oakes Ames (R, MA) and James Brooks (D, NY) were censured for their part in the Credit Mobilier scandal. Rep. Ames, who was a stockholder in Union Pacific and Credit Mobilier, a joint stock company related to the railroads, tried to bribe several politicians, including Rep. Brooks and House Speaker James Blaine (R, ME). In exchange for supporting railroad subsidies, they were to receive stock in Credit Mobilier. Efforts to expell the members failed (*Congressional Ethics: History, Facts, and Controversy*, 1992, pp. 7–10).

SENATOR DENNIS DECONCINI (D, AZ). See Keating Five.

REP. CHARLES DIGGS (D, MI). Rep. Charles Diggs was convicted on twenty-nine felony counts for "diverting more than $60,000 in employees' salaries to his personal and office use" (*Congressional Ethics: History, Facts, and Controversy*, 1992, p. 38). The following July the House voted to censure Diggs for the same activities. Diggs admitted to wrongdoing in exchange for dropping the investigations and calling for a censure instead of expulsion. A resolution to expel Diggs was debated but tabled. Diggs was sentenced to a maximum of three years in prison and resigned from the House in 1980 after initially planning to seek reelection (*Congressional Ethics: History, Facts, and Controversy*, 1992, pp. 38–39).

SENATOR THOMAS J. DODD (D, CT). Senator Thomas J. Dodd was censured by the Senate in 1967 for using campaign dollars for personal use. He had also been accused of double billing travel expenses and improperly exchanging favors. The ethics committee had recommended censure for the double billing, but the recommendation did not pass. In 1970 he sought reelection as an independent and lost. This was the first case investigated by the Senate ethics panel (*Congressional Ethics: History, Facts, and Controversy*, 1992, pp. 30–31).

REP. WALTER FLOWERS (D, AL). See Koreagate.

REP. TOM FOLEY (D, WA). See Koreagate.

REP. BARNEY FRANK (D, MA). Rep. Barney Frank was reprimanded in 1990 for using his office to help a male prostitute, Steve Gobie. Rep. Frank used his position to fix Gobie's parking tickets and wrote a letter to help Gobie get off of probation. Although the House ethics panel did not find that Frank used undo pressure in these matters, they thought the letter "could be perceived as an attempt to use political influence" (quoted in *Congressional Ethics: History, Facts, and Controversy*, 1992, p. 44). Some members on the ethics committee wanted a lighter sentence and some House members wanted censure or expulsion. Votes on the tougher actions easily failed. Frank was a committee chair at the time and a censure vote would have cost him his chairmanship. In the end Frank was reprimanded and required to pay the parking tickets (*Congressional Ethics: History, Facts, and Controversy*, 1992, pp. 43–44).

SPEAKER NEWT GINGRICH (R, GA). Rep. Newt Gingrich first faced charges of unethical behavior as a junior member from Georgia. While he was making accusations against then Speaker James Wright he was accused but acquitted of several different violations, ranging from failing to disclose a financial transaction, to misusing House stationary, to an inappropriate book deal (see *Congressional Ethics: History, Facts, and Controversy*, 1992, pp. 79–81). More significant, in 1997 Rep. Gingrich was distinguished by his colleagues as the first Speaker to be reprimanded. The final charge was failure to behave in a "manner that reflects credibly on the House" and stemmed from his misleading the Committee on Standards of Official Conduct. The committee had investigated charges that he illegally declared donations used for political purposes as tax exempt. In letters to the committee, Gingrich provided misinformation. The whole process was seen as partisan and led to a series of counter claims (Carr, 1997a, 1997b; Koszczuk, 1997).

SENATOR JOHN GLENN (D, OH). See Keating Five.

REP. WILLIAM J. GRAVES (W, KY). In 1838, Reps. William Graves and Henry Wise (Tyler D, VA) were not disciplined by the House for their role in the death of another member, Jonathan Cilley (Jackson D, ME). Cilley "had made statements on the floor reflecting on the character of James W. Webb, prominent editor of a New York City newspaper which was a Whig organ" (*Congressional Ethics*, 1980, p. 166). Graves went to see Cilley with a note from Webb, which led to a duel between Graves and Cilley that resulted in Cilley's death. Rep. Wise was a second in the duel. A vote was taken in the House to expel Graves but it failed, and a vote to censure Wise also failed. Since dueling was common at the time, several members did not believe these members should be disciplined (*Congressional Ethics*, 1980, p. 166).

REP. RICHARD HANNA (D, CA). See Koreagate.

REP. WAYNE HAYS (D, OH). In 1976, Rep. Wayne Hays, chair of the then powerful House Administration Committee and chair of the Democratic National Congressional Committee, resigned from the House as the Committee on the Standards of Official Conduct investigated whether he had put a mistress on his committee's payroll. Hays denied the allegations at first but then admitted to hiring her personally to be his mistress. Although the House ethics committee along with the FBI were investigating the allegations, the committee took no action after Hays announced his resignation from his leadership positions and eventually the House (*Congressional Ethics*, 1980, p. 22).

REP. ANDREW HINSHAW (R, CA). Although Rep. Andrew Hinshaw was convicted of bribery in 1976 and sentenced to jail, the House failed to expel him. Even the ethics committee voted against expulsion. Part of the reason no disciplinary actions were taken may have been that he lost his reelection bid in 1976. He was convicted of accepting bribes during his campaign. He later was also convicted of petty theft and misappropriation of funds (*Congressional Ethics*, 1980, pp. 23–24).

REP. JON HINSON (R, MS). Rep. Jon Hinson was reelected to Congress with 39 percent of the vote after admitting that he had been arrested for committing an obscene act. A year later he resigned after being arrested for attempting oral sodomy in a Capitol Hill men's room ("Hinson Resignation," 1981, p. 385).

HOUSE BANKING SCANDAL. In September 1991, the General Accounting Office reported that over 8,000 checks had bounced at the House bank between June 1989 and June 1990. The House voted immediately to close the bank and investigate it. It is difficult to interpret the meaning of the kited checks. The House bank did not operate like a normal bank and no tax dollars were involved. Members did not receive interest, and the bank at times was slow in depositing checks and lax in informing members about overdrafts. Some members were unaware that there had been overdrafts in their accounts. On the other hand, some members clearly took advantage of the poor bookkeeping, in effect giving themselves interest-free loans for campaigns and personal use by floating checks. After the House committee investigated the bank, it cited 22 members as having abused their banking privileges. The decision on which members abused the bank was based on how often they had been overdrawn by a significant amount. Although only these 22 members and former members were cited, 279 members and former members had at least one overdraft and 36 had bounced upwards of 100 checks in the roughly three-year period examined by the committee ("Voters Enraged," 1992, pp. 23–42).

REP. JOHN JENRETTE (D, SC). See Abscam.

KEATING FIVE. In 1991, the Senate reprimanded Senator Alan Cranston (D, CA) for his role in the Keating Five scandal. The scandal involved five senators who were accused of accepting campaign contributions from Charles Keating, a banker, to put undue pressure on the bureaucracy to help the Lincoln Savings and Loan. The other senators involved were Dennis DeConcini (D, AZ), John Glenn (D, OH), Donald Reigle (D, MI), and John McCain (R, AZ). Keating was convicted of securities fraud. Robert S. Bennett was hired as special counsel to investigate the scandal. He encouraged the ethics panel and the Senate to use the "appearance standard": Even if a member did not behave improperly they could be disciplined if it appeared improper. The ethics panel did not use the appearance standard but nevertheless rebuked four of the members for their behavior and reprimanded Cranston. According to the committee, Cranston "engaged in an impermissible pattern of conduct in which fundraising and official activities were substantially linked" (*Congressional Ethics: History, Facts, and Controversy*, 1992, p. 140) (*Congressional Ethics: History, Facts, and Controversy*, 1992, chap. 10).

REP. WILLIAM KELLEY (R, PA). In 1882, after Rep. John Daugherty White (R, KY) accused Rep. William Kelley of making and breaking a deal with whiskey distillers, the following exchange was made on the floor of the House:

Mr. White: It is merely a question of veracity. I heard him make the statement myself.

Mr. Kelley: And I denounce the statement as the ravings of a maniac or a deliberate lie.

Mr. White: The gentleman may be scoundrel enough to make that statement. (*Cong. Rec.*, 1882, p. 4904)

The language of the exchange was thought to be "disorderly and destructive of the dignity and honor of the House" (*Cong. Rec.*, 1882, p. 4904) and a motion to censure both men was made. After both members explained why they made the comments and apologized, the motion was dropped (*Cong. Rec.*, 1882, pp. 4896–4907).

KOREAGATE. Koreagate stemmed from a Justice Department investigation of corruption in Congress. The Korean government and Tongsun Park, a rice salesman, were accused of trying to bribe members of Congress. Two wives of House members, for example, reported receiving envelopes full of cash on a trip to Korea. Although they returned the money, two former members, Rep. Otto Passman (D, LA) and Rep. Richard Hanna (D, CA), were indicted on charges of bribery. Although Passman was eventually acquitted, Hanna was sentenced to two years in prison. Three Democratic members from California who were still in the House in 1978 were reprimanded for their role in Koreagate: Reps. John McFall (D, CA), Edward Roybal (D, CA), and Charles H. Wilson (D, CA). McFall was accused of receiving $4,000 to use House stationery to send letters on Tongsun Park's behalf to the Korean President Park. Reps. Roybal and Wilson were accused of misleading the House investigation. Wilson also failed to report, and then converted to personal use, a $1,000 cash campaign contribution made by Korean interests. In addition to those officially condemned, other members were implicated in the scandal. Reps. Tom Foley (D, WA), Walter Flowers (D, AL), Tip O'Neill (D, MA), and John Brademas (D, IN) were thought to have acted on Park's behalf and received campaign donations from him. Rep. Edward Patten (D, NJ) was also accused of accepting Korean cash campaign contributions and turning them into personal funds ("House Probes," 1977, pp. 820–825; *Congressional Ethics: History, Facts, and Controversy*, 1992, pp. 41–42).

SENATOR JOHN McCAIN (R, AZ). See Keating Five.

REP. JOHN MCFALL (D, CA). See Koreagate.

REP. WILBER MILLS (D, AR). In 1976, Rep. Wilber Mills resigned his chairmanship of the Ways and Means Committee and retired from Congress. Shortly before being reelected in 1974 Mills was stopped by the police for speeding. He appeared intoxicated and a stripper named Fanne Foxe left his car and jumped into the Potomac River. Later he was seen dancing with her in a Boston burlesque. These events harmed his reputation and he was later treated for alcoholism (*Congressional Ethics: History, Facts, and Controversy*, 1992, pp. 88–89).

REP. JOHN MURPHY (D, NY). See Abscam.

REP. JOHN MURTHA (D, PA). See Abscam.

REP. MICHAEL "OZZIE" MYERS (D, PA). See Abscam.

REP. TIP O'NEILL (D, MA). See Koreagate.

THE PAGE SEX AND DRUG SCANDAL. In the early 1980s, the Committee on Standards of Official Conduct investigated allegations of members taking drugs and having sexual relations with pages. The investigation resulted in two members being censured. Rep. Gerry Studds (D, MA) admitted to having a sexual relationship with a seventeen-year-old male page, while Rep. Daniel Crane (R, IL) had sexual relations with a seventeen-year-old female page. Both pages were of legal age in Washington, DC and the committee only recommended reprimanding the members since no crime had been committed. Rep. Newt Gingrich (R, GA) and Rep. Robert Michels (R, IL) felt a reprimand was too lenient and on the floor made a motion to censure the members. That motion carried. These are the only two cases of censure for sexual misconduct, although many members facing such accusations resigned or lost reelection when allegations were made. The investigation also resulted in drug charges for other members ("Two Members," 1983, pp. 580–583).

REP. OTTO PASSMAN (D, LA). See Koreagate.

REP. EDWARD PATTEN (D, NJ). See Koreagate.

REP. ADAM CLAYTON POWELL, JR. (D, NY). In 1967, the House took the unusual step in excluding Rep. Adam Clayton Powell, Jr. Rep. Powell, chair of the Education and Labor Committee, had numerous allegations of wrongdoing brought against him. He had had problems with the Internal Revenue Service, and although he was not convicted of tax evasion he was forced to pay back taxes and penalties. He was sued for libel and then fined for hiding property to avoid paying the libel judgment. He had the House pay for pleasure trips and put his wife on his payroll, even though she lived in Puerto Rico. He had also so alienated the Education and Labor Committee that the committee voted to increase subcommittee chairs' powers to bring bills to the floor. After winning reelection in 1966 the House voted not to seat him in the 90th Congress (voted for exclusion). He was also fined $40,000, lost his chairmanship, and lost his seniority. The exclusion was later held unconstitutional by the Supreme Court (*Congressional Ethics*, 1980, pp. 153–155).

SENATOR DONALD REIGLE (D, MI). See Keating Five.

REP. DAN ROSTENKOWSKI (D, IL). In 1994, Rep. Dan Rostenkowski was indicted on seventeen felony counts for having ghost employees, converting stamps bought with government funds into cash, and using taxpayer monies and campaign funds to buy cars, personal items, and gifts, but pleaded guilty to just two counts of mail fraud and received a jail sentence of seventeen months. At the time he was chair of the Ways and Means Committee and considered one of the most powerful members of the House. He was also known as a member who grew up with the spoils system in Chicago and was willing to use the perks of office. In 1994 he lost his reelection bid and the House never disciplined him (Cloud, 1994b; Kuntz, 1994a, 1994b).

REP. EDWARD ROYBAL (D, CA). See Koreagate.

REP. ROBERT SIKES (D, FL). In 1976, Rep. Robert Sikes was reprimanded for financial misconduct. He was chair of the House Military Construction Appropriations Subcommittee and failed to disclose on his financial disclosure forms that he owned stock in Fairchild Industries and First Navy Bank. It was also felt that it was a conflict of interest for him to own the stock in the bank. After the reprimand he lost his chairmanship and resigned from the House in 1978. Sikes was the first member investigated by the House Committee on the Standards of Official Conduct (*Congressional Ethics*, 1980, p. 22).

REP. GERRY STUDDS (D, MA). See page sex and drug scandal.

REP. FRANK THOMPSON (D, NJ). See Abscam.

REP. JAMES TRAFICANT, JR. (D, OH). In 2002, Rep. James Traficant Jr. became the fifth member to be expelled from the House. Even before entering Congress, Traficant had had legal problems. In 1981 he was indicted and later acquitted of racketeering. It was alleged that as sheriff he accepted mob money. This made him a bit of a hero in the Youngstown area. In his ninth term as a House member he was convicted of ten federal charges, including tax evasion, racketeering, bribery, and fraud. He apparently took kickbacks from staff, had them work on his farm (without pay), and accepted free labor and gifts from businesses in exchange for lobbying on their behalf. In both of his trials he served as his own attorney, even though he is not a trained lawyer (Singer, 2002).

REP. JOHN DAUGHERTY WHITE (R, KY). See Rep. William Kelley.

REP. B. F. WHITTEMORE (R, SC). In 1870, Rep. B. F. Whittemore resigned from the House before it could vote to expel him on charges that he sold cadetships to West Point and the Naval Academy in violation of the law. Rep. Whittemore was subsequently reelected to the House and a motion in the same Congress was passed not to seat him. During the debates there was much discussion on whether the House had a legitimate role in not letting the voters select their preferred candidate (*Congressional Globe*, 1870, pp. 4669–4674).[1]

REP. CHARLES H. WILSON (D, CA). See Koreagate.

REP. HENRY WISE (TD, VA). See Rep. William Graves.

SPEAKER JAMES WRIGHT (D, TX). In 1989, Speaker Jim Wright resigned from the House amid allegations of an illegal book deal, excessive influence peddling, and favors Wright received from a wealthy constituent. With the book deal, Speaker Wright had lobbyists purchase a book he wrote to avoid the honorarium ban and filter money to his personal account. The influence peddling involved Wright using his power to help out a savings and loan. When it appeared as though he might be disciplined, he resigned (*Congressional Ethics: History, Facts, and Controversy*, 1992, pp. 20–23).

NOTE

1. The *Congressional Globe* was the precursor to the *Congressional Record*.

References

Abramson, P., Aldrich J. H., & Rohde, D. (1987). Progressive ambition among United States senators: 1972–1988. *Journal of Politics, 49*, 3–29.

"Abscam" scandal clouded Congress' image. (1980). *Congressional Quarterly Almanac, 35*, 513–525.

Alford, J., Teeters, H., Ward, D. S., & Wilson, R. K. (1994). Overdraft: The political cost of Congressional malfeasance. *Journal of Politics, 56*, 788–802.

Angle, M. (1992). Voters may not "clean the House," but a good dusting is certain. *Congressional Quarterly Weekly Reports, 50*, 2785–2786.

Ansolabehere, S., Iyengar, S., & Simon, A. (1999). Replicating experiments using aggregate and survey data: The case of negative advertising and turnout. *American Political Science Review, 93*, 901–910.

Ansolabehere, S., Iyengar, S., Simon, A., & Valentino, N. (1994). Does attack advertising demobilize the electorate? *American Political Science Review, 88*, 829–838.

Baker, R. A. (1985). The history of Congressional ethics. In B. Jennings & D. Callahan (Eds.), *Representation and responsibility: Exploring ethics* (pp. 3–27). New York: Plenum Press.

Banducci, S. A., & Karp, J. A. (1994). Electoral consequences of scandal and reapportionment in the 1992 elections. *American Politics Quarterly, 22*, 3–26.

Barone, M., Ujifusa, G., & Matthews, D. (various years). *Almanac of American politics*. Washington, DC: National Journal.

Bauer, R. F. (1998, March 9). Political resolutions needed for charges against the president. *Roll Call Month*, p. 9.

Beard, E., & Horn, S. (1975). *Congressional ethics the view from the House*. Washington, DC: The Brookings Institution.

Benson, G.C.S. (1978). *Political corruption in America*. Lexington, MA: Lexington Books.

Booth, W. (1997, Sept. 4). Jury convicts Symington in fraud case: Arizona governor to resign Friday. *Washington Post*, p. A1.

Brace, P. (1984). Progressive ambition in the House: A probabilistic approach. *Journal of Politics, 46*, 556–571.

Bresnahan, J. (2002, July 29). Threat derails ethics filing. *Roll Call, 48*, 1, 29.

Carey, J. M., Niemi, R. G., & Powell, L. W. (2000). *Term limits: In the state legislatures*. Ann Arbor: University of Michigan Press.

Carr, R. (1997a). Partisan rancor between leaders behind committee's problems. *Congressional Quarterly Weekly Reports, 55*, 155–159.

Carr, R. (1997b). Subcommittee lays out details of Gingrich ethics violations. *Congressional Quarterly Weekly Reports, 55*, 13–15.

Carter signs government-wide ethics bill. (1978). *Congressional Quarterly Almanac, 34*, 847.

Clark, K. (1997). Paying the price for heightened ethics scrutiny: Legal defense funds and other ways that government officials pay their lawyers. *Stanford Law Review, 50*, 65–138.

Cloud, D. (1994a). End of session marked by partisan stalemate. *Congressional Quarterly Weekly Reports, 52*, 2847.

Cloud, D. (1994b). Rostenkowski guilty plea closes corruption saga. *Congressional Quarterly Weekly Reports, 52*, 980.

Cohen, L., & Copeland, G. (August 1997). *Congress reviled: Support for term limits in the American electorate*. Paper presented at the annual meeting of the American Political Science Association, Washington, DC.

Congressional districts in the 1970s. (1973). Washington, DC: Congressional Quarterly.

Congressional districts in the 1980s. (1983). Washington, DC: Congressional Quarterly.

Congressional districts in the 1990s: A portrait of American. (1993). Washington, DC: Congressional Quarterly.

Congressional ethics (2d ed.). (1980). Washington, DC: Congressional Quarterly.

Congressional ethics: History, facts, and controversy. (1992). Washington, DC: Congressional Quarterly.

Congressional globe. (1870). 41st Cong., 2d sess., pt. 4: 4669–4674.

Congressional quarterly almanac. (various years). Washington, DC: Congressional Quarterly.

Congressional record. (1882). 47th Cong., 1st sess., 13, pt. 4: 4896–4907.

Congressional record. (1977). 95th Cong., 1st sess., 123, pt. 5: 5896–5951.

Connor, G. E., & Oppenheimer, B. I. (1993). Deliberation: An untimed value in a timed game. In L. Dodd & B. I. Oppenhiemer (Eds.), *Congress reconsidered* (4th ed., pp. 315–330). Washington, DC: CQ Press.

Copeland, G. W. (1983). When Congress and the president collide: Why presidents veto legislation. *Journal of Politics, 45*, 696–710.

Crabtree, S. (2002, May 16). Cheney aides deny conflict of interest. *Roll Call, 47*, 1.

della Porta, D. (2000). Social capital, beliefs in government, and political corruption. In S. Pharr & R. D. Putnam (Eds.), *Disaffected democracies: What's troubling the trilateral countries?* (pp. 202–230). Princeton, NJ: Princeton University Press.

della Porta, D., & Vannucci, A. (1997). The "perverse effects" of political corruption. *Political Studies, 45*, 516–539.

Dillman, D. A. (1978). *Mail and telephone surveys: The total design method*. New York: John Wiley & Sons.

Dimock, M. A., & Jacobson, G. C. (1995). Checks and choices: The House bank scandal's impact on voters in 1992. *Journal of Politics, 57,* 1143–1159.

Doherty, C. J. (1998). All in a day's battle: McCain, the eager warrior. *CQ Weekly, 56,* 1356–1359.

Durr, R. H., Gilmour, J. B., & Wolbrecht, C. (1997). Explaining Congressional approval. *American Journal of Political Science, 41,* 175–207.

Eakins, K. R. (March 2002). *Ambition and role orientation of lawyers and non-lawyers in the Ohio legislature.* Paper presented at the Southwestern Social Science Association, New Orleans, LA.

Easton, D. (1986). An approach to the analysis of political systems. In I. Kabashima & L. White III (Eds.), *A world politics reader: Political system and change* (pp. 23–40). Princeton, NJ: Princeton University Press.

Elazar, D. J. (1972). *American federalism: A view from the states* (2d ed.). New York: Thomas Y. Crowell.

Feldman, M. (2002, October 24). Clean state, dirty politicians. *New York Times,* p. 35.

Fenno, R. F. (1973). *Congressmen in committees.* Boston: Little, Brown.

Fisher, S. H., III, & Herrick, R. (2002). Whistle while you work: Job satisfaction and retirement from the U.S. House. *Legislative Studies Quarterly, 27,* 445–459.

Francis, W. L., & Kenny, L. W. (1996). Position shifting in pursuit of higher office. *American Journal of Political Science, 40,* 768–786.

Frantzich, S. (1978). Opting out: Retirement from the House of Representatives. *American Political Science Quarterly, 6,* 251–273.

Frantzich, S. (1979). Who makes our laws? The legislative effectiveness of members of the U.S. Congress. *Legislative Studies Quarterly, 4,* 409–428.

Friedman, E., Johnson, S., Kaufman, D., & Zoido-Lobaton, P. (2000). Dodging the grabbing hand: The determinants of unofficial activity in 69 countries. *Journal of Public Economics, 76,* 459–493.

Garment, S. (1991). *Scandal: The culture of mistrust in American politics.* New York: Times Book Random House.

Gephardt, R. (1999). *An even better place: America in the 21st century.* New York: Public Affairs.

Gettinger, S. (1998). Here's one bill Gingrich wants no part of. *CQ Weekly, 56,* 1194.

Getz, R. S. (1966). *Congressional ethics: The conflict of interest issue.* Princeton, NJ: D. Van Nostrand.

Gilligan, C. (1982). *In a different voice: Psychological theory and women's development.* Cambridge: Harvard University Press.

Ginsberg, B., & Shefter, M. (1990). *Politics by other means: The declining importance of elections in America.* New York: Basic Books.

Goldstein, K., & Freedman, P. (2002). Campaign advertising and voter turnout: New evidence for a stimulation effect. *Journal of Politics, 64,* 721–740.

Grenzke, J. M. (1989). PACs and the Congressional supermarket: The currency is complex. *Legislative Studies Quarterly, 4,* 409–428.

Groseclose, T., & Krehbiel, K. (1994). Golden parachutes, rubber checks, and strategic retirements from the 102d House. *American Journal of Political Science, 38,* 75–99.

Hall, R. L., & Wayman, F. W. (1990). Buying time: Moneyed interests and the mobilization of bias in Congressional committees. *American Political Science Review, 84,* 797–820.

Harris, F. R. (1995). *In defense of Congress*. New York: St. Martin's Press.

Hastings Center. (1985). *The ethics of legislative life*. New York: Hastings Center.

Herrick, R. (2000). Who will survive? An exploration of factors contributing to the removal of unethical House members. *American Politics Quarterly, 28*, 96–109.

Herrick, R., & Moore, M. K. (1993). Political ambition's effect on legislative behavior. *Journal of Politics, 55*, 765–776.

Herrick, R., Moore, M. K., & Hibbing, J. R. (1994). Unfastening the electoral connection: The behavior of U.S. representatives when reelection is no longer a factor. *Journal of Politics, 56*, 214–227.

Herrick, R., & Nixon, D. L. (1996). Is there life after Congress? Patterns and determinants of post-Congressional careers. *Legislative Studies Quarterly, 21*, 489–499.

Heywood, P. (1997). Political corruption: Problems and perspectives. *Political Studies, 45*, 417–436.

Hibbing, J. R. (1982). *Choosing to leave: Voluntary retirement from the U.S. House of Representatives*. Washington, DC: University Press of America.

Hibbing, J. R. (1991). Contours of the modern Congressional career. *American Political Science Review, 85*, 405–429.

Hibbing, J. R., & Theiss-Morse, E. (1995). *Congress as public enemy: Public attitudes toward American political institutions*. New York: Cambridge University Press.

Hinson resignation. (1981). *Congressional Quarterly Almanac, 37*, 385.

Hook, J. (1989). Speaker draws battle lines in fight for political life. *Congressional Quarterly Weekly Report, 47*, 789–792.

Hook, J. (1994). Judgment calls on a career: The Rostenkowski vigil. *Congressional Quarterly Weekly Report, 52*, 1359–1361.

House Probes Korean Influence—Buying Plot. (1977). *Congressional Quarterly Almanac, 33*, 820–825.

Jamieson, K. H., & Falk, E. (2000). Continuity and change in civility in the House. In J. R. Bond & R. Fleisher (Eds.), *Polarized politics: Congress and the president in a partisan era* (pp. 96–108). Washington, DC: CQ Press.

Jacobson, G. C. (1997). *The politics of Congressional elections* (4th ed.). New York: Longman Press.

Jacobson, G. C., & Dimock, M. A. (1994). Checking out: The effects of bank overdrafts on the 1992 House elections. *American Journal of Political Science, 38*, 601–624.

Kane, P. (2002, July 18). Torrecelli hits $3 million mark in payouts to lawyers. *Roll Call, 48*, 10.

Katz, J. L. (1998). Livingston straddles Republican fault line as he hunts for votes for speaker's job. *CQ Weekly, 56*, 979–984.

Kiewiet, R. D., & Zeng, L. (1993). An analysis of Congressional career decisions, 1947–1986. *American Political Science Review, 87*, 928–941.

Kimball, D. C., & Patterson, S. C. (1997). Living up to expectations: Public attitudes toward Congress. *Journal of Politics, 59*, 701–729.

Kohlberg, L. (1984). *Essays on moral development: Vol. 2. The psychology of moral development: The nature and validity of moral stages*. San Francisco: Harper & Row.

Koszczuk, J. (1997). Republicans struggle to leave ethics probe behind them. *Congressional Quarterly Weekly Reports, 55*, 226–229.

Koszczuk, J., & Weisman, J. (1997). Gingrich's path to a comeback is strewn with obstacles. *Congressional Quarterly Weekly Reports, 55*, 825–827.

Kuntz, P. (1992). Overdrafts were a potent charge. *Congressional Quarterly Weekly Reports, 50*, 3575.

Kuntz, P. (1994a). Rostenkowski on trial: Assessing the charges. *Congressional Quarterly Weekly Reports, 52*, 1439–1446.

Kuntz, P. (1994b). A scion of the spoils system. *Congressional Quarterly Weekly Reports, 52*, 1445.

Leeper, M. S. (1991). The impact of prejudice on female candidates: An experimental look at voter inference. *American Politics Quarterly, 19*, 248–261.

Lichter, S. R., & Amundson, D. R. (1994). Less news is worse news: Television news coverage of Congress, 1972–1992. In T. E. Mann & N. Ornstein (Eds.), *Congress, the press and public* (pp. 131–140). Washington, DC: American Enterprise Institute and the Brookings Institution.

Locke, E. A. (1983). The nature and causes of job satisfaction. In M. D. Dunnett (Ed.), *Handbook of industrial and organizational psychology* (pp. 1297–1350). New York: Wiley.

Mauro, P. (1995). Corruption and growth. *Quarterly Journal of Economics, 110*, 681–707.

Mauro, P. (1997). The effects of corruption on growth, investment, and government expenditure: A cross country analysis. In K. A. Elliott (Ed.), *Corruption and the global economy* (pp. 83–108). Washington, DC: Institute for International Economics.

Mayhew, D. R. (1974a). *Congress: The electoral connection.* New Haven: Yale University Press.

Mayhew, D. R. (1974b). Congressional elections: The case of the vanishing marginals. *Polity, 6*, 295–317.

Mayhew, D. R. (1991). *Divided we govern: Party control, lawmaking, and investigations, 1946–1990.* New Haven: Yale University Press.

McCurley, C. M., & Mondak, J. J. (1995). Inspected by #1184063113: The influence of incumbents competence and integrity in U.S. House elections. *American Journal of Political Science, 39*, 864–886.

Mintz, E. (1996). Members' roll call attendance sets election-year record. *Congressional Quarterly Weekly Reports, 54*, 3439.

Mondak, J. J. (1995). Competence, integrity and the electoral success of Congressional incumbents. *Journal of Politics, 57*, 1043–1070.

Neal, T. M. (1998, December 11). At USDA event, Espy is portrait of triumph: Former secretary's acquittal cheered. *Washington Post*, p. A29.

Ornstein, N. J., Mann, T. E., & Malbin, M. J. (2000). *Vital statistics on Congress 1999–2000.* Washington, DC: Congressional Quarterly.

Parker, G. R. (1996). *Congress and the rent-seeking society.* Ann Arbor: University of Michigan Press.

Patterson, K. D., & Magleby, D. B. (1992). The polls—poll trends public support for Congress. *Public Opinion Quarterly, 56*, 539–551.

Patterson, S. C., & Barr, M. K. (1995). Congress bashing and the 1992 Congressional election. In H. F. Weisberg (Ed.), *Democracy's feast: Elections in America* (pp. 263–291). Chatham, NJ: Chatham House.

Patterson, S. C., & Caldeira, G. A. (1990). Standing up for Congress: Variations in public esteem since the 1960s. *Legislative Studies Quarterly, 15*, 25–46.

Peaden, C., & Herrick, R. (November 2001). *Citizen Coburn: A study of rotation in Congressional office*. Paper presented at the annual meeting of the Oklahoma Political Science Association, Stillwater, OK.

Peters, J. G., & Welch, S. (1980). The effects of charges of corruption on voting behavior in Congressional elections. *American Political Science Review, 74*, 697–708.

Polsby, N. (1968). The institutionalization of the House of Representatives. *American Political Science Review, 62*, 146–168.

Rieselbach, L. N. (1994). *Congressional reform: The changing modern Congress*. Washington, DC: CQ Press.

Roberts, R. N., & Doss, M. T., Jr. (1997). *From Watergate to Whitewater: The public integrity war*. Westport, CT: Praeger.

Robinson, M. J. (1994). The three faces of Congressional media. In D. A. Graber (Ed.), *Media power in politics* (3d ed., pp. 248–263). Washington, DC: CQ Press.

Rogers, E. M., & Dearing, J. W. (1988). Agenda-setting research: Where has it been, where is it going? In J. A. Anderson (Ed.), *Communication yearbook 11* (pp. 555–594). Newbury Park, CA: Sage.

Rohde, D. W. (1979). Risk-bearing and progressive ambition: The case of the United States House of Representatives. *American Journal of Political Science, 23*, 1–26.

Roll Call. (various years). Washington, DC: Congressional Quarterly.

Rosenthal, A. (1996). *Drawing the line: Legislative ethics in the states*. Lincoln: University of Nebraska Press.

Rundquist, B., Strom, G. S., & Peters, J. (1977). Corrupt politicians and their electoral support: Some experimental observations. *American Political Science Review, 71*, 954–963.

Sabato, L. J. (1991). *Feeding frenzy*. New York: Free Press.

Sabato, L. J., & Simpson, G. R. (1996). *Dirty little secrets*. New York: Times Books.

Sapiro, V. (1981–1982). If U.S. Senator Baker were a women: An experimental study of candidate image. *Political Psychology, 3*, 61–83.

Schlesinger, J. A. (1966). *Ambition and politics: Political careers in the United States*. Chicago: Rand McNally.

Schmidt, S. (1997, December 3). Probe of O'Leary over charity donation ends. *Washington Post*, p. A33.

Schmidt, S. (1998, February 21). Ex-Governor to cooperate with Starr, Tucker plea bargains in Whitewater case. *Washington Post*, p. A1.

Seligson, M. (2002). The impact of corruption on regime legitimacy: A comparative study of four Latin American countries. *Journal of Politics, 64*, 408–433.

Singer, P. (2002, April 12). Traficant convicted in corruption case. *Tulsa World*, p. A8.

Soule, J. W. (1969). Future political ambition and the behavior of incumbent state legislators. *Midwest Journal of Political Science, 13*, 439–454.

Stark, A. (1997). Beyond quid pro quo: What's wrong with private gain from public office? *American Political Science Review, 91*, 108–120.

Stewart, C., III. (1994). Let's go fly a kite: Correlates of involvement in the House bank scandal. *Legislative Studies Quarterly, 19*, 521–535.

Thompson, D. (1995). *Ethics in Congress: From individual to institutional corruption*. Washington, DC: The Brookings Institution.

Tyler, T. R. (1990). *Why people obey the law*. New Haven: Yale University Press.

Two members censured. (1983). *Congressional Quarterly Almanac, 38*, 580–583.

U.S. House Committee on Rules. (1997). Revisions to the rules of the House and the rules of the Committee on Standards of Official Conduct, 105th Cong., 1st sess, 4 March and 20 June.

Verba, S., Schlozman, K. L., & Brady, H. E. (1995). *Voice and equality: Civic voluntarism in American politics.* Cambridge: Harvard University Press.

Voters enraged over House bank abuses. (1992). *Congressional Quarterly Almanac, 48,* 23–42.

Wave of diversity spared many incumbents. (1992). *Congressional Quarterly Almanac, 48,* 15-A–24-A.

Wawro, G. (2001). A panel probit analysis of campaign contributions and roll-call votes. *American Journal of Political Science, 45,* 563–579.

Wayne, L. (1997, January 26). A special deal for lobbyists: A getaway with lawmakers. *New York Times,* p. 1.

Welch, S., & Hibbing, J. R. (1997). The effects of charges of corruption on voting behavior in Congressional elections, 1982–1990. *Journal of Politics, 59,* 226–239.

Williams, S., & Lascher, E., Jr. (Eds.). (1993). *Ambition & beyond: Career paths of American politicians.* Berkeley, CA: Institute of Governmental Studies Press.

Wilson, H. H. (1951). *Congress: Corruption and compromise.* New York: Rinehart.

Worchel, P., Hester, P., & Kopala, P. S. (1974). Collective protest and legitimacy of authority. *Journal of Conflict Resolution, 18,* 37–54.

Wright, J. R. (1985). PACs, contributions, and roll calls: An organizational perspective. *American Political Science Review, 79,* 400–414.

Index

ABOUT THE AUTHOR

Rebekah Herrick is Associate Professor of Political Science at Oklahoma State University. Her teaching and research interests include congressional behavior, congressional elections, and gender and politics. She has published in a variety of scholarly journals, including *American Politics Quarterly, Journal of Politics, Legislative Studies Quarterly, Social Science Journal*, and *Women & Politics*.